THE CIVIL WAR IN AMERICA

ALAN BARKER was born in Edinburgh and educated at Jesus College, Cambridge, where he received his B.A. in 1941 and M.A. in 1949. He was an Assistant Master at Eton College from 1947 to 1958 and was given a Commonwealth Fund Fellowship to Yale in 1951–52. It was there that he started work on THE CIVIL WAR IN AMERICA. He was a Fellow of Queens' College, Cambridge, and Director of Studies in History from 1953 to 1955, and since 1958 he has been Head Master of The Leys School, Cambridge. Mr. Barker has contributed to *The Times Literary Supplement* and is one of the authors of the *General History of England 1688–1960*.

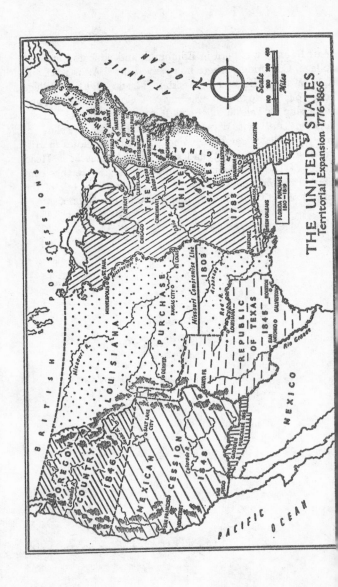

THE UNITED STATES
Territorial Expansion 1776-1866

THE CIVIL WAR IN AMERICA

BY

ALAN BARKER

Anchor Books
Doubleday & Company, Inc.
Garden City, New York

PREFACE

he origin and purpose of this book is threefold. It started
om a series of lectures delivered at the University of Cam-
idge in 1955; these appeared to be welcomed by under-
aduates reading American History, as providing some guide,
wever rough, to the vast literature on the Civil War. Then at
on in 1956 it was decided to have the Civil War as a special
bject, but no book of the right size seemed to exist. The first
lf of the present book thus came to be written as an intro-
ction to the subject. Finally I was stimulated to finish the
ok by the interest of friends in a subject which is overwritten
America (particularly as the Centenary has approached)
d greatly underwritten in England.

Rash as it is to trespass on ground so well covered by experts,
s perhaps even more rash to try to appeal in the same book
readers among the general public, the universities and the
ools. I believe, however, that the American Civil War is one
the most fascinating and satisfying studies in all History,
l that a short introduction to it is much needed. I hope that
ne of my readers will find it useful and that the subject may
ve to them, as it has proved to me, one of abiding interest.

I am greatly indebted to my wife, and to Professor H. C.
en, Mr. Barnaby Benson, Dr. Robert Birley, Mr. D. J.
aham-Campbell, Miss Margaret Haferd, Mr. C. P. Hill, Mr.
H. Hinsley, Dr. H. C. Porter and Mr. C. H. Wilson for ad-
e of various kinds; and to my colleague Mr. M. F. Howard
reading the proofs. I must record my gratitude to the Com-
nwealth Fund of New York for enabling me, through a
rkness Fellowship, to spend a year studying American His-
y at Yale University, and also to Queens' College, Cam-

bridge, within whose friendly walls the main work on this book was done.

ALAN BARKER

THE LEYS SCHOOL
October 1960

'Let us have faith that right makes might; and in that faith let us, to the end, dare to do our duty as we understand it.'

ABRAHAM LINCOLN

'The question is, whether it is right; and if it is right, I take the responsibility.'

ROBERT E. LEE

Exegi monumentum aere perennius.

Contents

Maps

THE CIVIL WAR IN AMERICA

CHAPTER I

THE IMPORTANCE OF THE AMERICAN CIVIL WAR

John Morley considered the American Civil War as 'the only war in modern times as to which we can be sure, first that no skill or patience of diplomacy would have avoided it, and second that the preservation of the American Union and the abolition of Negro slavery were two such vast triumphs by which even the inferno of war was justified'. Such confidence in judgement is rare on this subject, which has occupied the minds and pens of thousands of scholars, publicists, journalists and novelists. As early as 1866 John Russell Bartlett could publish a book on *The Literature of the Rebellion* containing several thousands of items. Since then the number has run into tens of thousands; there can be no aspect of the subject which has not been touched upon. Yet even with all this writing, all this investigation, it is often difficult to escape from the cry in Robert Southey's poem *The Battle of Blenheim*:

> 'Now tell us what 'twas all about',
>   Young Peterkin he cries;
> And little Wilhelmine looks up
>   With wonder-waiting eyes;
> 'Now tell us all about the war
>   And what they fought each other for.'

> 'It was the English', Kaspar cried,
>   'Who put the French to rout;
> But what they fought each other for,
>   I could not well make out.'

Like Kaspar we know the outcome of the battle. In the American Civil War the North was militarily victorious, the independence of a Southern Confederacy was prevented and Negro slavery was legally abolished by constitutional amendment. But on almost every other subject to do with the war—its causes, its leaders, its course—we often find ourselves agreeing with Albert Beveridge who, in the middle of writing his life of Lincoln, exclaimed that 'the examination of source materials has well nigh dazed me since they revealed the truth to be exactly the contrary to the teachings of my youth'. This is the common experience of those who have learnt their history from the necessary generalizations of text-books and who at some time in their life have the leisure to explore the events in detail. It is the object of this short book to encourage such exploration. There could be no more salutary lesson for a student of the Civil War than to examine, for example, the origin and nature of the Kansas-Nebraska Act of 1854. Only by such an examination will he discover the extremely prejudiced nature of the accounts given in many books.

Perhaps because so many differing views are taken of the American Civil War, the fact remains that it continues to be the most popular historical subject in American history. It is the one which excites the most interest, the most acrimony and the most research. Northerners and Southerners continue to reveal deep and strongly felt prejudices about it. American interest in the subject is comparable to the woman who discusses her operations, describes her symptoms and elaborates the difficulties of her convalescence. No other nation except France has a subject of such abiding interest. In a sense it is true that the French Revolution of 1789 and the American Civil War are refought in every decade because the issues which were involved in them are vigorously alive in the present day. Militarism, clericalism and the reconciliation of liberty with order are issues which have disturbed every French régime since 1789 and which exercise the consciences of individual Frenchmen. To the Americans the Civil War tested their achievement of independence and proved that a republican government, 'the world's best hope', could endure. It marked the triumph of nationalism over states' rights. It was concerned with matters of prime importance to the present day —Negro rights, the power of the President and the power of the Congress over him. F. D. Roosevelt earned the same abuse as Lincoln over his use of Presidential prerogatives; while Congress, if it has never gone as far as it did in the decade after the Civil War, has sought constantly to extend its power. Attempts by Congress in the Presidency of Harry S. Truman to limit the President's control of foreign policy; the senatorial filibusters over civil rights bills; the action of President Eisenhower in sending Federal troops to Little Rock in face of the state Governor's invocation of states' rights on the issue of Negro education: all these incidents of the recent past are evidence that the issues of the Civil War period are still of vital concern today. From the Civil War, too, emerged modern industrial America, whose problems and achievements engage the interests of the world.

Not only are the issues still alive, but the visible memorials of the epic struggle are there for all to see. The battlefields of Gettysburg, Fredericksburg, Chickamauga (to name but a few), and the forts which defended Washington against the threat of Lee's army are preserved as symbols of the great American achievement. In almost every Southern town stands a memorial to the Confederate dead in the 'war between the states', paralleled in New England by the memorials commemorating the dead in the 'war of the Rebellion'. These historical remains are all the more important since in the United States historical monuments are few. Aldous Huxley has shrewdly commented that for the European 'the greatest charm of travel in the New World is the high ratio of its geography to its history'. The reverse is true for travel in Europe where, within a single city, architectural evidence of several political systems (and even civilizations) can be found. In Italy the Romans, Goths, Germans, Spanish and French have all left their mark in marble, stones or brick. A visitor to Ravenna can only ponder on the variety and unpredictability of human history: it would show a rash confidence to feel that any permanence was possible. By contrast America has relatively few monuments. Discounting Indian relics, the only evidences of civilization before the Anglo-Saxons are the occasional Spanish Mission houses in California and New Mexico and the French squares in New Orleans. Neither Spain nor France really occupied America, and the reminders they have left are a sign of what might have been. Instead Americans have memorials to what has been: the hall in Philadelphia where the Declaration of Independence was signed; the monument at Concord where 'once the embattled farmers stood, and fired the shot heard round the world'; the fortifications of Yorktown from which the British General emerged in October 1781 to surrender his army. The constitution designed by the Founding Fathers is still in being today and an American looking around him is reassured of the inevitability of the particular kind of society in which he lives and of its form of government. The monuments of America stand for the destiny of a chosen people. Even those of the Civil War reinforce this impression since they stand as a sign not of the disruption but of the continuity of the American tradition. They are not memorials to the uncertainty and chance of political systems, nor to the rise and fall of great theories of society. They commemorate rather the period in which the American experiment of republican government was tested and not found wanting.

The Civil War came at a time when Europe was in a period of revolution. The struggle of Liberals against the autocrats who had triumphed in 1848, the Risorgimento in Italy, and the Paris Commune were all evidence of a conflict between rival theories of society. The Civil War in America had no direct connection with this wind of change blowing through the continent of Europe. This is not to say that Europeans were not interested in it, nor that in a wider sense certain fundamental human rights were not involved. Lincoln saw the worldwide issue clearly; it was simply to prove false the words which John Adams, the second President, had spoken in the first decade of the Republic: 'Remember democracy never lasts long. It soon wastes, exhausts and murders itself. There never was a democracy that did not commit suicide.' Jefferson, the third President, had answered this challenge in his Inaugural Address by declaring his faith in the American form of government as 'the world's best hope'. 'Sometimes,' he continued, 'it is said that man cannot be trusted with the government of himself. Can he then be trusted with the government of others? Or have we found angels in the forms of kings to govern him? Let history answer this question.' Lincoln in hi

Gettysburg address stated the same faith in imperishable form. 'Four score and seven years ago our fathers brought forth on this continent, a new nation, conceived in Liberty, and dedicated to the proposition that all men are created equal. Now we are engaged in a great civil war, testing whether that nation, or any nation so conceived and so dedicated can long endure.' Put in this way the American contest obviously was of profound significance to Liberals in Europe, where the tide of reaction was fast flowing in favour of absolutism. Typical of the interest taken was that of John Bright, the famous Manchester Liberal, and Karl Marx, an exile in London whose articles on the war showed how little it fitted into the context of European socialism.

Despite the international significance of the American Civil War, it had also a character uniquely American. It was a conflict between two regions, distinctly and geographically separate, which had existed for over seventy years within a Federal system of government. This system had, with its checks, balances and compromises, worked on the whole reasonably well until the gulf between the two regions had become too wide to be adequately bridged. Neither the North nor the South was dissatisfied with the existing constitution in theory: they merely disagreed over its interpretation. Each claimed to be defending the authentic original constitution, and the South, when it seceded from the Union, adopted no new constitution for the Confederacy. It retained the old one with certain modifications designed to secure those rights which it believed the North had perverted. Alexander Stephens, the Vice-President of the Confederacy, in his book *Constitutional View of the late War between the States*, based his justification on an appeal to the meaning of the original constitution. Even the North, in the last few years before the Civil War when faced by the Supreme Court decision over Dred Scott, produced no new theory. If the Court by its legal decision supported the Southern claims, then an appeal had simply to be made to the authentic revolutionary tradition contained in the Preamble to the Declaration of Independence. The letter of the law must give way to the spirit.

Neither side in fact enunciated any new political theory. The

constitution of the United States had come into being through
a compromise between the powers granted to the Federal government and those retained by the individual states. Compromise was at the heart of the American political tradition and
Civil War only came with deadlock after a long series of compromises on many issues. The South as a backward agricultural
area was seeking to maintain an interpretation of states' rights
which was valid in terms of the original Union. Her conception of the constitution was static. The North, on the other
hand, was really claiming that the Union was a dynamic or-
ganism changing with geographical expansion, industrial advance and immigration. In such a Union the national or Federal
power must be superior to the individual state. Yet the interesting fact is that Northern politicians advanced this argument
in essentially conservative terms. They argued not so much that
the Union had changed as that the constitution itself envisaged
the growth of the Federal power. The argument in both cases
was legalistic, based on an existing constitution, not on a new
one.

The same conservative approach can be seen in the arguments advanced before the Civil War about the type of society
in North and South. Both sides claimed to be entirely satisfied
with conditions as they existed. Publicists in the North praised
their society for its prosperity and growth, pointing to the backwardness of the South in contrast. The South, for its part, condemned the grasping materialism of Northern life and asked
that all aspects of Southern life should be looked at. If this
were done, they argued, slavery could be seen in its proper
context and the virtues of Southern society would be properly
revealed. The writings of the Southerners, Thomas Dew and
George Fitzhugh, contained essentially an appeal to facts, just
as *Uncle Tom's Cabin* rested on a body of evidence collected
about slavery. What is, is also what ought to be. Nowhere do
we find an appeal to some vision of an ideal society as can be
found, for example, in the French Revolution by the Girondin
or in the Spanish Civil War by the Republicans. Both North
and South went to war in 1861 to defend the type of society
which already existed in those regions. This conservatism is

unique and is closely paralleled by the political conservatism of the constitutional arguments.

Even when the North eventually won its overwhelming military victory, no overwhelming revolution occurred socially or constitutionally. The bitter experience of Radical Reconstruction in the South did not destroy Southern society. If anything, it helped to emphasize white domination over the Negro, and in defeat the South cast a romantic glow over the traditional values of life in 'Dixie'. Down to the present day, even with the recent growth of industry, parts of the South remain economically backward. Politically, the triumph of the North did not mean that the constitution was rewritten. Three constitutional amendments freed the slave and attempted to secure full civil and political rights to the Negro. But otherwise the constitution remained untouched. In practice the national emphasis in the constitution was henceforth established and has grown more pronounced with the years, yet in theory the states retain their sovereign power. Only a superficial observer of American affairs would underestimate the importance of the areas within which state power is still paramount.

The tradition of compromise still remained as the key to American life after the Civil War. The United States emerged from the bloodiest Civil War in history with its political tradition unimpaired. This is a unique phenomenon and is evidence of the essentially conservative nature of the conflict. The fact that the nation could survive the ordeal of Civil War seemed to prove the strength of the thread which bound the present to the past. It proved also the manifest destiny of the United States; that a chosen people could expand across a continent within a constitutional structure designed by the Fathers of the Republic. If ever proof was needed that these Founding Fathers were inspired, the survival of the Union from the years of Civil War provided more than sufficient.[1]

Americans and students of American history find the Civil War fascinating both because it was concerned with issues that are still alive today and because it confirms so much of

[1] A full discussion of the American political tradition can be found in Daniel J. Boorstin's brilliant essay, *The Genius of American Politics*.

the American political tradition. But there is a third reason
which makes the Civil War of interest to any historian. This
is the problem of the cause of war. Twentieth-century man is
more interested in this problem than were any of his predecessors in centuries when war was neither total nor all-destructive.
Quite apart from any practical considerations, the investigation
of the cause of a war focuses the difficulty of the historian's
task more directly than any other historical exercise. It brings
the historian face to face with the possibilities and nature of
his craft. Interpretation is always both a challenge and a risk.
As Sir Isaiah Berlin has pointed out in his essay on *Historical
Inevitability* the risks often frighten the men best equipped to
interpret, leaving the fools to rush in. Moreover in the past
hundred years theories have been current, which, if accepted,
allow for no interpretation of historical events in terms of individual responsibility at all. One such theory is that of deter-
minism. The assumption here is that all human action is determined by impersonal forces of one kind or another—classes,
the spirit of the age, scientific laws or vague historical trends.
Individuals are no more than swimmers floating with the tide.
In so far as they appear to have influence on events, they will
be doing so only in so far as they are co-operating with the
inevitable force, class, spirit or what you will.

Another theory can be called that of pessimism. The argument here runs that the historian must always be so ignorant
of the past, however hard he researches, that he can never begin to catch a glimpse of the truth. The most he can hope to
do is to uncover a small portion of the vast intricate canvas of
the past and he is in no position to generalize, attribute blame
or hold individuals responsible. Men knew not what they did
and the historian can neither hope to discover what really occurred nor what was intended.

Neither of these two theories allows the historian to interpret human events as actions in which individual men and
women played a decisive part. Sir Isaiah argues that such a
denial runs counter to human nature, to our ordinary everyday behaviour and conversation. We do not refrain from judgement in our personal life, and the historian, however much
he may like to do so, must not refrain from interpretation and

judgement on the past. Despite deeper causes individual men took decisions which brought war. Individual responsibility cannot be shelved on to circumstances, racial movements or sectional conflict. It may be, as Professor Butterfield has suggested, that the universal tendency of man to sin exerts a 'gravitational pull' on events which brings the best intentions to ruin. Men indeed know not what they do when they make a decision; but they know what they intend. A host of individual decisions—some selfish, others altruistic—may so arrange events that a war becomes inevitable after a particular further action. It is somewhat similar to those gambling machines in which a certain number will win the jackpot. The machinery is set, a coin is inserted and the machine begins to move. The person who inserted the coin is powerless to change the outcome; the gears and the cog wheels have been set in motion by the coin. So it is with an event like the assassination of the Archduke Franz Ferdinand in 1914, the throwing of Martinitz and Slavata from the Hradschin Palace in 1618 or the sending of a relief expedition to Fort Sumter in 1861. An individual inserted the coin and individuals played their part by personal decisions in arranging the pattern of events from which a war comes. Chance does enter in; the jackpot comes up but rarely. Yet in looking at the causes of any great conflict it is possible to disentangle some of the individual decisions which help to set the machinery in such a position that the jackpot can come up. At least with an event like the beginning of a great war, we are in a better position than the priest in Thornton Wilder's *Bridge of San Luis Rey* who sought to find the reason why a particular strand of rope broke at a particular time.

American historians have given a host of causes for the outbreak of the Civil War. They range from conspiracy and human wickedness to climate, conflicting civilizations, self-righteousness and political ambition. The approach to the problem is exactly similar to that shown by European historians to the causes of the 1914 war. After this war to end war, men demanded an explanation of why it had occurred. Periodicals appeared dedicated to research on the subject; special institutes were established and almost every great power published lengthy volumes of diplomatic documents. More detail is known about the events between June 28th and August 4th, 1914, than about any other five weeks of history, and as Mr. A. J. P. Taylor has observed, if we cannot understand these events and come to some decision about them we shall never understand or decide about anything. The same is true of the American Civil War and the research that has been done about it. The pattern of explanation too has been similar. At first it centred on the events which followed the election of Lincoln (assassination of the Archduke Franz Ferdinand). Then the investigation was carried further back. The South blamed the alliance of the North and West. (The Germans blamed the Franco-Russian alliance of 1894.) The North blamed the policy of successive Democratic Presidents from Andrew Jackson in 1832. (The French blamed the policy of Bismarck though he left office in 1890.) Others blamed sectional rivalry, constitutional antagonisms, the moral fervour of the abolitionists, the activities of expansionist Southerners (in Europe paralleled by the structure of alliances, the armaments race, capitalist imperialism, the power of the press and the growth of stereotyped views of other nations). The trouble of all such general theories is that they will explain almost anything one wants explained. There is little point in seeking the reasons why war came in 1861 or 1914. A more fruitful enquiry is why the factors which had so long preserved peace failed to do so ultimately.

The historian of any war is faced by a multitude of events, facts and people. The only way to discipline this multitude is to ask certain questions. The first one is, 'Where do I begin?' and it is as well to avoid the error of John W. Draper, who in his *American Civil War* spent 350 of his 634 pages in dealing with geography, the Negro in Africa, the colonization of America, the white man in Europe, the change from Roman to Gothic architecture, and the Saxon invasion of England. A second question is, 'What is the relationship of immediate episodes to underlying forces?' Can episodes such as the Dred Scott decision, John Brown's raid, and the relief of Fort Sumter be called causes of war? A further question is, 'What influence did individuals exert on events?' Yet even questions like these are not altogether helpful. In trying to interpret the causes of the American Civil War a more profitable line of approach is to divide the whole problem into three. What were the causes of sectional conflict? What were the causes of secession? What were the causes of war? It is wrong to assume (as it is so easy to do with the advantage of hindsight) either that sectional conflict meant secession or that secession meant war.

We have to assume, as does any practising historian, that there is a certain pattern of cause and effect in history. The effects are often likely to be different from those intended by their authors. Men may have their actions conditioned by circumstances, yet the belief in freedom of choice and voluntary action is so fundamental to us that any interpretation of history which does not allow for this is plainly unsatisfactory. If we believe this, the American conflict was neither inevitable nor irrepressible.

In considering the causes of the Civil War it is a mistake to think that increased knowledge necessarily brings increased understanding. Despite the vast body of research on every aspect of the war, the explanations of the war put forward today are astonishingly similar to those advanced by the earliest writers on the subject. A book by Thomas J. Pressly called *Americans interpret their Civil War* has traced with bibliographical tenacity the differing views that have been held. A shorter and more stimulating approach to the subject can be found in David Potter's lecture, 'The Lincoln Theme and American National Historiography.' Three main periods of interpretation exist; the first lasted approximately up to 1880, the second till 1918 and the third from 1918. In the first period interpretations of the war were purely sectional. Northern writers put the guilt firmly on the shoulders of the South: the conflict was the result of a gigantic conspiracy of Southern slave owners, and the main issue of the war was slavery. The murder of Lincoln produced a deep emotional upheaval in the North. As Potter puts it:

> He became the object of fabulous tales such as had hardly been told since the days of the monastic chroniclers, and national legend began to endow him with qualities that one would associate with the hero of a saga. In

epic terms such as Homer might have used, this legend stressed his great physical strength, coupled with the tenderest compassion for the weak, his brooding wisdom, his infinite patience and humility. Soon it raised him to a level which surpasses the human altogether and partakes of the divine. Hence emerged a figure born in a log-cabin as lowly as any manger, growing up to bear the sorrows of the race and to suffer for all humanity. At last, on Good Friday, 1865, his life on earth was sacrificed for the redemption of the Union, and on Easter Sunday the people met in churches throughout the land to mourn the Saviour of the States.

This legendary picture of Lincoln underlies all the writing which viewed the Civil War as a great moral drama between slavery and freedom, state sovereignty and nationalism. As an interpretation of the war, it reaches its climax in the *Constitutional and Political History of the United States* by Hermann von Holst.

In the South there was a similar unity of sentiment. Jefferson Davis and Alexander Stephens were not alone in placing war guilt firmly on the North. The South had a constitutional right to secede in face of the aggressive policy of the North. Slavery was no more the cause of the war than money in a bank is the cause of the bank being robbed. Southerners also argued that the Confederacy was a nation fighting for its liberty:

> *No nation rose so white and fair*
> *Or fell so pure of crimes.*

The South was full at this time of apologists whose arguments have been well summed up in the words put into the mouth of an imaginary orator commemorating the Confederacy:

I shall relate briefly the outstanding events of the period during which the Constitution of the United States was drafted; then I shall trace the pernicious development, and expose the fallacy, of John Marshall's theory of nationalism, and I shall vindicate beyond all cavil the right of secession. From that I shall pass to the events of the war and shall pay tribute to General Lee, to General Jackson and to the private soldier, and I shall conclude of course with a tribute to Southern womanhood.

Apart from these Northern and Southern interpretations which regarded the war as inevitable there was also a less publicized interpretation which regarded the conflict as a needless one. Just as the attitudes of North and South were born in the furnace of war, so this interpretation stemmed from the discontented men throughout the United States who had disliked the war throughout its course. Northern Democrats and Constitutional Unionists had opposed the war and from their attitudes arose a third interpretation of the conflict. This argued that sectional strife and conflict had arisen from artificial issues fanned and emotionalized by extremists in both North and South. Abolitionists and Southern nationalists had prevented compromises; both parties had been wrong and misguided and the nation had blundered into a needless war.

After 1880, when Radical Reconstruction was ended and the immediate passions had cooled, a new view of the conflict arose. This emphasized the achievement of the war in preserving the American Union. The war was seen as a triumph of nationalism. The courage and sacrifice of the two sides were praised while the whole question of guilt was minimized. Both sides must share part of the blame but neither should bear the whole responsibility. Forces beyond the control of men had much to do with making the conflict inevitable and despite the cost in blood and suffering, the eventual outcome—the maintenance of the Union—was a good one. This approach was most fully elaborated in *The History of the Civil War, 1861–1865*, by James Ford Rhodes. The self-satisfaction which coloured this view of the war received a blow from the writings of certain economic historians of whom Charles and Mary Beard are the most renowned. They held that the Civil War had radically and calamitously altered the nature of American government and society. The conflict had been a total disaster which enabled Northern capitalism to re-design American life and society in its own image. The protest was not simply confined to history books but appeared in a political form in the

platform of the Populist party in 1892. The Populist movement
was essentially a protest from agricultural America.

> We meet [the preamble to the platform read] in the
> midst of a nation brought to the verge of moral, political
> and material ruin . . . the fruits of the toil of millions are
> boldly stolen to build up colossal fortunes for a few, un-
> precedented in the history of mankind; and the possessors
> of these, in turn, despise the Republic and endanger lib-
> erty. From the same prolific womb of governmental in-
> justice, we breed the two great classes—tramps and mil-
> lionaires.

This was the gravamen of the charge made against the Civil
War by the Beards. Despite it, however, the nationalist interpretation remained in favour down to the First World War.

These four main interpretations—pro-Southern, pro-North-
ern, the needless war, and the economic attack—have continued to appear in various forms in the past forty years. Historians like U. B. Phillips and F. L. Owsley elaborated an
enthusiastic defence of the South. The emphasis changed to
the factor of race. Slavery was a system of race relationship
which served to keep the South a white man's country. Although Southern life before the war was not perfect, it had
many attractions and advantages. Given time, the question of
slavery would have been solved. The Civil War did not destroy
the problem of race in the South and it really created more
problems than it solved. The South had not wanted the war
which was the result of the selfish aggression of an industrial
North. Under the influence of the two world wars the school
of historians who had regarded the war as both unnecessary
and avoidable received great support. J. G. Randall and Avery
Craven are the two greatest historians in this tradition and
their lead was followed by W. E. Woodward and E. M. Coulter. They believed that war, in any form, was always useless,
never settling any issue in a sensible fashion. It was the worst
possible method of dealing with relations between men. Looking at the American Civil War, they could find no irreconcilable differences between North and South in the pre-war decades, and they denied that there was a development of two

diverse civilizations. Blame rested with ambitious politicians, newspaper editors and the abolitionists, all of whom emphasized the superficial differences rather than the fundamental common interests of the sections. Owing to their activities the people in North and South gained a distorted picture of each other; they were never confronted with realities or the fundamental issue. The nation therefore blundered into war without knowing what it was all about. If the leaders had been honest war could have been avoided; men would have realized that their disagreements were not worth fighting about. Properly led, men would have remained unemotional and realistic. The state of psychological tension which ultimately welcomed war would never have arisen. Articles with the title, 'The Civil War, a National Blunder', 'The Years of Madness', 'When we went crazy' illustrate this view only too well. To historians of this tradition Stephen Douglas, the compromiser, the Northern Democrat, was the real hero rather than Lincoln, the President, whose refusal to compromise caused the final crisis. G. F. Milton's *Eve of Conflict*, published in 1934, was the first favourable defence of Douglas as a realist and a man of sense. Before this the Illinois senator had always been condemned as a man of limited moral sense and wavering political standards.

If this view of regarding the Civil War as avoidable is a product of the World Wars, it can be argued that those historians who disagreed with it were inspired by the failure of the European appeasers to prevent war in 1939. Dwight L. Dumond has emphasized the moral problem of slavery which it was impossible for men of conscience to avoid. The most convincing attacks, however, have come in two articles, one by A. M. Schlesinger, Jr., the other by the Dutch historian, P. Geyl. Schlesinger in 'The Causes of the Civil War; a note on Historical sentimentalism', in Volume XVI of the *Partisan Review*, demands that historians face up to the moral issue of slavery. Randall, he argues, by ignoring it and by dismissing impatiently the handful of abolitionists, cannot hope to understand the period. Geyl is even more outspoken. He agrees that the American people found themselves in a war which the great majority on both sides did not want. But he denies that this is proof that the war might have been avoided; it is rather proof of the general proposition that the course of history is not arranged by the conscious will of the majority. Jefferson Davis showed great shrewdness when he remarked, 'Neither current events nor history show that the majority rules or ever did rule. The contrary I think is true.' According to Geyl, Randall's view of a generation blundering into war ignores the overwhelming moral problem of slavery out of which the Civil War came. As a problem it could never be posed in absolute terms, but that does not mean it did not exist. Randall never sees this issue. Because the majority would have preferred to ignore it, this does not mean that they were right. Geyl goes on to charge Randall with making a deceptive distinction between artificial and fundamental causes of the war. 'He counts among artificial causes everything that does not agree with the wishes of the majority and with its true interests defined by himself in accordance with the best rational standards. He ignores the non-rational factors of passion, emotion, conviction, prejudice and misunderstanding.' Geyl's point is well made: if Randall does not ignore these factors he undoubtedly gives them too little weight. It is precisely these factors which bring crises in the affairs of men. The ordinary citizen is seldom rational and finds it only too easy to follow the lead of others.

So the battle of interpretation over the American Civil War continues to rage almost as hotly today as it did in the generation after the war. Increased knowledge has not altered the viewpoint but has simply added material for the argument. The most recent synthesis of the whole matter has been the four volumes by Allan Nevins (*Ordeal of the Union* and *The Emergence of Lincoln*). Nevins appears to try to get the best of both worlds. He feels that the war should have been avoidable yet welcomes the triumph of the Union. Critics have attacked him for 'being blinded by his sense of moral values' and also for never 'giving the moral value full weight'. His four volumes are, however, beyond question the most authoritative and readable account of the years before the Civil War broke out.

Any survey of historical writing about the Civil War shows that however objective an historian may claim to be, his prejudices, his philosophy of life and his circumstances will affect his outlook on the causes and consequences of this mighty struggle. This is a truism, but in an age when so much is said about historical objectivity it is worth a moment's reflection. An historian's categories are not neutral as are those of a chemist or a physicist. He is a human being dealing in human categories and he cannot describe the great events of the past without implying that certain individuals may have caused them. As Sir Isaiah Berlin has argued, the claim of the historian to be scientific springs 'from a desire to resign our responsibility, to cease from judging provided we are not judged ourselves and above all are not compelled to judge ourselves'. In this context the American Civil War has an importance beyond an interest in American history or in the cause of war. Any study of its causes drives us back to considering the role of the individual's responsibility in any great crisis of human affairs. In democratic countries with a well-founded adult franchise, it should not be possible to transfer the blame to elected leaders. If great wars are not inevitable they can only be prevented by the continuing interest of individual voters in the affairs of the day. The ordinary citizen of the United States before the Civil War did not possess this interest; he was too concerned with his own affairs, too ready to believe what he was told and too eager to bury his head in the sand.

However difficult the study of a great war may be, it is undoubtedly one of the most challenging for the historian. Lincoln, in his Second Inaugural Address as President in 1865, gave his own explanation of the coming of the war. 'On the occasion corresponding to this four years ago all thoughts were anxiously directed to an impending Civil War. All dreaded it . . . all sought to avert it. . . . Both parties deprecated war, but one of them would *make* war rather than let the nation survive, and the other would *accept* war rather than let it perish, and the war came.' 'And the war came.' Lincoln in these words was recognizing that the Almighty has his own purposes but he was not accepting an attitude of fatalism that men were powerless to prevent the war. If a great catastrophe in the Christian view of history is in some sense a judgement on a particular society, this does not mean that the judgement would have come if men had acted differently. Individual decisions and actions led to sectional conflict; sectional conflict led on to secession, and secession to war by similar individual actions. A study of how this happened gives an opportunity of seeking historical truth within a limited field. The American Civil War is sufficiently distant in time, neatly limited in its scope and involved with relatively simple issues so as to provide the ideal experiment for unravelling the causes of war. Though no final answers can be found, the search for them must only be profitable to anyone concerned with individual responsibility in the affairs of men.

CHAPTER II

THE BACKGROUND OF THE WAR

(i) *The Constitution and Political Parties*

The constitution provided the framework within which the conflicts culminating in the Civil War were fought. Moreover, many people have argued that the war itself was caused by rival interpretations of the original constitution. In understanding the background, therefore, of the Civil War, it is necessary to glance at the main principles underlying the American constitution. It is equally important to understand the character of American political parties. During most of the history of the Republic these parties have been nation-wide, drawing support from every section of the country. By 1860, however, this national character of the parties had ceased to exist owing to the pressures of the previous two decades. The strain imposed by slavery on the political system of the United States, in fact, blinded men to the many common interests which should have held the Union together. The Civil War was the outcome of this blindness.

The constitution emerged from the dissatisfaction felt with the Articles of Confederation (1781) by which the original thirteen states had established a form of common government for themselves. Although this government did not deserve all the criticisms levelled against it both by contemporaries and by later historians, it was undoubtedly designed to prevent the existence of a strong central authority. The inability of enforcing a strong policy at home or abroad stimulated a group of far-sighted men into seeking means of improving co-operation between the states. Congress was inspired to summon representatives from all the states in February 1787 'for the sole and express purpose of revising the Articles of Confederation'. This Constitutional Convention began its work in May 1787 at Philadelphia and on September 17th it completed its labours, which resulted in a new constitution rather than in a revision of the Articles. This new constitution would become effective when it had been ratified by nine states, and so it was not until April 30th, 1789, that George Washington was inaugurated as First President.

In the circumstances of the time, when a man's loyalty was primarily to his state, it was impossible for the constitution-makers to design a national government, which men like Alexander Hamilton would have preferred. As one of them said, 'the only chance we have to support a general government is to graft it on to the state governments'. The resulting constitution was therefore the outcome of compromise carried through in the sweltering heat of the summer. A Federal government was set up with the *executive* power given to a President; a *legislature* divided into two houses, the Senate where all states irrespective of size were equally represented, a House of Representatives where representation went by population; and a *judiciary* whose powers were vague until the famous Chief Justice John Marshall established its authority as the arbiter of the constitution. The powers of the Federal government were strictly defined in its executive and legislative branches and the vital power of taxation and the regulation of commerce was granted. Within its defined sphere the Federal power was supreme and it acted directly on the individual citizen without the mediation of the state. Each state retained all those powers not specifically granted to the Federal government, but certain matters were particularly prohibited to them, such as entering into a treaty of alliance or levying duties on trade.

The basis of this compromise was the written constitution establishing a rule of law for the new Republic which could only be changed by a complicated process of amendment. The overriding concern was to prevent tyranny arising at any one point; hence the checks and balances. The President and the two houses of Congress were to be elected at different times by different people; the President had a veto on Congress but his veto could be overridden by a two-thirds majority; the Senate shared the President's power of making treaties and appointments. Within their own spheres the individual states remained supreme; only within the limits specified by the constitution had the Federal government any power to act. To deal with any uncertainty in this matter the 10th Amendment (the last of those passed in 1791 to reassure opinion hostile to the constitution) stated that 'the powers not delegated to the United States by the Constitution, nor prohibited by it to the states, are reserved to the states respectively or to the people'. Thus did the people of the United States agree to the document designed 'to form a more perfect union, establish justice, insure domestic tranquillity, provide for the common defence, promote the general welfare, and to secure the blessings of liberty' to themselves and their posterity. Nothing was said of what would happen if a state or states felt that these purposes were not being fulfilled; it was presumed that the intricate machinery of the constitution would protect the interests of everyone.

The majority of the constitution-makers were men of property, seeking a stable government which would secure credit, assist trade and establish the prestige of the United States among the nations of Europe. For almost all of them had their eyes turned eastwards to Europe and their vision of the new Republic was based on an English model. Their ideal was a strong and efficient government controlled by the propertied class. As realists they had little faith in human nature and believed that liberty, property and union depended on an aristocracy of the wise, the good and the rich. This creed was fundamentally the same as that of the small ruling class in England during the 18th century. Even the reforming influence of the Whigs after 1783 was directed primarily at strengthening the power of the aristocracy against the Crown. Three thousand miles across the Atlantic the American Revolution had not destroyed this ideal of government but its reality had been undermined by the radical element (particularly from the western regions of the seaboard states) which had taken the opportunity of the quarrel with England to attack the fundamental position of the propertied class in America. The new constitution was a conservative move against the radicals, and the constitution-makers hoped that the United States would now settle down. The last thing they expected was the rise of political parties. The most that was expected was the kind of division which had existed between groups of the English Whigs of the 18th century. Thus the machinery constructed in the constitution for the election of the President made no allowance for a contest between candidates of opposed parties.[1]

But these expectations were stillborn. Thomas Jefferson, a Virginian who was the American Minister in France at the time of the Constitutional Convention, soon showed that his vision for the United States was inspired by very different ideas from those of the Federalists (as the supporters of a strong government modelled on English lines came to be called). He believed that America, 'the world's best hope', should turn its back on Europe and, with the unparalleled opportunities before it, seek its own destiny free from the entanglements which Europe involved. He rejected the idea of an aristocracy. To Jefferson the ideal America was a nation of farmers governing themselves, with a Federal government exercising the minimum of influence. Individuals should do things for themselves; the government's job was merely to preserve law and order, not to initiate schemes of internal improvements and banking.

On his return from France Jefferson became Secretary of State in Washington's Cabinet but he soon found himself out of sympathy with most of his colleagues. He resigned his office and became the focus for an opposition party called the Democratic Republicans (or Democrats for short)[2] composed of the idealists, the radicals and the malcontents. Yet actually it

[1] The procedure of election by the electoral college still exists, but the 12th Amendment, passed in 1804, established separate ballots for the President and the Vice-President.

[2] The name was originally Republican in order to emphasize the character of the party in contrast to the monarchical tendencies among the Federalists. Democrat was a word of abuse at the time, equivalent to the word Bolshevik in the 1920's. An American in the 1790's described a Democratic society as 'that horrible sink of treason, that hateful synagogue of anarchy, that odious conclave of tumult, that hellish school of rebellion and opposition to all regular and well balanced authority'. After the defeat of the Federalists in 1800, Democrat, from being a term of abuse, became a term of honour, and was used to describe the party of Jefferson.

was an event in Europe which finally crystallized the American political parties. This was the French Revolution. To the American conservatives the French upheaval typified everything they had dreaded from their own revolution and, although the Atlantic and not merely the Channel separated them from Paris, their horror was as great as that of their English counterparts. For twenty-five years the American political scene was dominated by Europe; newspapers devoted the bulk of their space to foreign events; the stage adopted political themes, vituperation was translated into European terms and the wheelings and manœuvres of the Federalists and Democratic parties were dictated by events on the Rhine, Danube or in the English Channel. The climax of this party conflict came with the defeat of Adams for the Presidency in 1800. With the Democrats in power and with the extension of the United States westwards by the Louisiana Purchase of 1803, the Federalist strength steadily declined until its undignified expiry in the secessionist movement of New England in 1814.[3] America now turned her back on Europe and concentrated on the problems raised by her westwards expansion. Party lines did not exist in the period after 1815, known as the 'era of good feelings' and politicians ranged themselves behind individual leaders like Henry Clay, J. Q. Adams and Andrew Jackson. Around these men, politicians manœuvred to advance the interests of their locality, and out of these forces two new political parties emerged whose dominance lasted until the Civil War.

The 1828 Presidential election brought General Andrew Jackson to the White House at the head of a new Democratic party. This party was compounded of many elements, as any American political party has had to be, once universal suffrage and an expanding Union had replaced the ideal of a European state ruled by the good, the rich and the wise. In Jackson's two terms as President the modern American political system emerged. With universal manhood suffrage existing in many states, a political machine able to turn out the votes at election time was required. Local issues would obviously matter most to the individual voter, particularly when he lived in the West

[3] See page 34.

where communities were isolated; but the task of the party machine was to organize these individual votes to obtain victory not only at the local, but also at the state and the national level. The 'spoils' system by which public offices, however small, were at the disposal of the victorious administration, allowed the loyal workers of the party to be rewarded for their services. The nominating convention, by which the party delegates from each state met together to decide on the party's candidate for the Presidency, prevented the possibility of votes being wasted on a variety of candidates. So successful was this convention system that it eventually became common practice in the selection of candidates for offices at levels less exalted than the Presidency.

This new political system admirably filled the needs of a Union which was steadily growing in size (1816 Indiana, 1817 Mississippi, 1818 Illinois, 1819 Alabama, 1820 Maine, 1821 Missouri, 1836 Arkansas, 1837 Michigan, 1845 Texas, Florida, 1846 Iowa). Just as the railways strengthened the ties between regions thousands of miles apart, so the political labels of two major parties harnessed a diversity of interests and ambitions into two organizations for wielding political power at the local and the national level. The second party, called the Whigs, had developed in opposition to the Jacksonian Democrats and in 1840 they succeeded in a spectacular way in winning the Presidency by methods directly borrowed from their rivals. It is always tempting to try and analyse the various interests, groups and classes making up these two political parties, but it is an impossible task. By the conditions of universal suffrage they had to appeal to as many people as possible and, in making this appeal, they were prepared to be all things to all men. Obviously on certain matters they had to make a stand, but the manœuvres of political leaders were usually delicate compromises trying to offend as few voters as possible. Each party was really a coalition of different local interests, seeking to capture the machinery of the Federal government to advance those interests. The main issues in the period from 1824 onwards were the tariff, the United States' Bank, the cost of buying Western lands and the validity of Federal funds being used to finance improved communications. It would be true to say that the Whigs, the heirs of the Federalists in many of their attitudes, favoured a Federal Bank, a high tariff and the use of Federal money to build roads and canals, financed by the sale of Western lands at a high price. The Democrats, on the whole, took the opposite view, some of them favouring no banks at all, others only local banks and the majority seeking the abolition of the tariff and the sale of Western lands at a cheap price. The Whigs therefore had the votes of business men, bankers and industrialists, of conservative plantation owners, of factory workers, whose livelihood depended on a high tariff, and of frontiersmen who wanted Federal aid for improving their communication system. The Democrats had the farm vote and the support of all those who wished to emigrate to the West and buy land easily. Involved in these issues was the vexed question of the powers of the Federal government as against those of the states. It is not cynical to observe that the Federal power was supported on the occasions when particular interests were seeking the benefits of Federal action; at other times the same interests were strong allies of state power.

But there is no simple key; the picture is that of a kaleidoscope. Whigs and Democrats in different localities did not often take the same view of matters as their fellow Whigs and Democrats in other parts of the country. Lincoln, who was the product of a humble pioneer home, was a Whig with little in common with the wealthy bankers and industrialists of the East. But he did believe that the powers of the national government should be used to develop all the nation's resources, whereas the basic belief of the true Jacksonian Democrat (as it had been that of the Jeffersonian Democrat) was that national government should be of the most limited and economical kind. If it were otherwise, the government would become the prey of competing factions seeking to use Federal power for local interests. Hence Jackson, in his Maysville Road veto of 1830, turned down the use of Federal funds for internal improvements on the grounds that such action was unconstitutional and that individual states should develop their own transport system. Many states attempted to do so, indulging in extravagant schemes floated on loans raised in New York or Europe. The result was the financial panic of 1837 which brought many such schemes to ruin.[4]

The resentment of many Westerners showed itself when they voted for the Whig party in 1840. Southern Democrats had supported Jackson in the hope that he would reduce the tariff; when he failed to do so, because the tariff provided the bulk of the Federal revenue, thus enabling Western lands to be sold cheaply, his Southern supporters challenged him directly in the Nullification controversy.[5] They resented a tariff which benefited the North-East and the cheap price for Western lands did not interest them. The Democratic party was far from harmonious and local interests, in matters of local concern, were not always satisfied with the ideal of a modest, economical government. Only over the Bank of the United States were Democrats of North, South and West united; this monopolistic concern, with its far-ranging tentacles, seemed to be of advantage only to the industrialists and bankers of the North-East, and Jackson had united support in his attack upon it. An issue like this would give coherence to the whole party; then it would break apart again, yet remain a national party— an uneasy coalition of different interests reconciled by a continual process of bargains and compromises. The Whig party was similarly constituted, believing broadly in the need for a strong national government in contrast to the Democratic belief in a simple government.

Only when the slavery question became of paramount concern (as we shall see) did the political kaleidoscope solidify into a definite unbreakable pattern. The aim of all politicians was to prevent this happening; they tried to distract attention from controversial issues, to keep conscience and principles out of politics and to maintain the national character of their parties. Democrats and Whigs in North, South and West differed on many points among themselves, but as long as slavery was not the main issue, they could mix within two political parties whose programmes were the result of compromise between

[4] In Illinois, for example, a debt of 17 million dollars was incurred for internal improvements at a time when the total states' budget was 57,891 dollars.
[5] See p. 35.

local interests. Compromise remained the secret of the successful working of a constitution whose creation had been the result of compromise. Distrust of a strong central authority had
also conditioned many of the clauses of the constitution and
this distrust remained as a permanent feature of American life.
The failure of compromise and the failure of strong leadership
combined by 1860 to bring about the Civil War.

(ii) *The Frontier and Sectionalism*

If the Founding Fathers did not expect the growth of political parties, neither did they visualize the staggering geographical growth of the United States. Even when Jefferson
acquired Louisiana from Napoleon (1803) he believed that
it would provide sufficient room for the expansion of a thousand years. Westward expansion had always been going on
but in the 19th century the pressure was greatly increased by
the flow of immigrants from abroad. In the following ten-year
periods the total number of immigrants were: 1800–10, 70,-
000; 1810–20, 114,000; 1820–30, 130,000. In the single year
1842 104,000 entered; in 1847 it was nearly a quarter of a million and in 1854 came 427,000, the highest figure before the
Civil War. The total result can be seen in the rise in the
American population from 5,308,000 in 1800 to 9,638,000 in
1820, 17,069,000 in 1840 and 31,443,000 in 1860. Since as
late as 1850 four-fifths of the people lived in towns of less
than 2,500 inhabitants, it is obvious that the vast spaces of the
West had absorbed a considerable proportion of the increasing population. The development of the frontier is a fascinating story of hope and tragedy, success and failure, opulence
and squalor. The hunters were followed by the vagrants, the
misfits from the East who for a time scraped a living from the
wilderness and then moved on, to be succeeded by the family
who intended to settle. Settlement required not only courage
and determination but also a certain amount of capital. Most
of the settlers were therefore seldom new immigrants from
Europe, who naturally congregated in the cities where a beg-
garly wage could be earned at once. Life on the frontier was

hard and often brutal. A savage climate brought bitter cold
and blazing heat; floods or a drought could ruin a year's work
and the desperate isolation of frontier farms meant that life or
death depended mainly on luck.

The story of Abraham Lincoln's family provides a good illustration in concrete form of Western expansion in America.
Abraham's grandfather was a prosperous farmer in Virginia
who moved into Kentucky in 1782. It was there that Lincoln
was born in 1809. Two years later his father moved to a new
farm near to the Cumberland trail from Louisville to Nashville where 'moved a restless eager cavalcade: pioneers with
rumbling wagons and driven livestock heading for the North-
West, peddlers who brought wares from the outside world,
itinerant preachers, now and then a coffle of slaves trudging
behind a mounted overseer or slave trader'. In 1816, having
lost money owing to a faulty land title, the family moved
again westwards to Indiana where settlement was light and
the Lincolns cleared their own plot in the wilderness. Their
fourteen years there were years of hardship, toil and disease,
breaking the spirit of Abraham's father, but impressing on the
son qualities of courage and perseverance. In 1827 the lure of
westward prosperity made Thomas Lincoln once more sell up
his property and embark in three wagons for Illinois, infinitely poorer than when he first left Kentucky in 1811.

Whatever the effect on personal fortunes of moving westwards as the frontier advanced, there is little doubt that con-
tact with the frontier profoundly affected ways of thought and
attitudes. Respect for convention and for established authority
was likely to decrease in the conditions of the wilderness. Class
lines were blurred as isolated farmers 'were forced by the endless crises of daily life to turn their hands to repairing firearms,
setting splints, arguing law cases, preaching sermons, keeping
law and order; and their womenfolk to teaching, making
clothes and delivering babies'. The Westerner was forced to
improvise and, though disasters might come and a drought or
a tempest might destroy his livelihood, those who survived
emerged with a new self-confidence. Attitudes to politics, to
religion, to law, to economics were all subtly altered by the
impact of the frontier; the American, whether a native-born

one or a European immigrant, became a new man in his advance to the West. Perhaps he remained a farmer or tried his hands at half a dozen occupations from tavern-keeper to stage-driver, but usually he felt that the good life lay in the West away from Europe and the East, that 'somewhere down the river, or over the next horizon, there would be found the perfect property, that idyllic way of life which all were seeking'.[6] American Western films provide a stereotype of life in the West but the best of them give a good idea of the roughness of life in a wooden farmhouse, the brutality of rough-and-ready law enforcement and the equality which frontier conditions encouraged.

Although life on the frontier varied considerably in different areas, it is worth taking as an illustration the life of Abraham Lincoln from when he left his family in Illinois. Until this moment he seemed condemned to the harsh life of laborious toil which had become the lot of his family. He left to sail a cargo of pork, corn and live hogs down river to New Orleans on behalf of a prosperous salesman. This was the second trip he had done in a flat boat, constructed with his companions from trees they felled, down the overhung shallows into the great waterway to become one of a large caravan of keelboats, steamboats and rafts, all carrying a wide variety of cargoes. On his return he became a salesman for his employer at New Salem, a small village of twenty-five families on the Sangamon River in Illinois. This was a typical pioneer community with a fluid population of a distinctly Southern tinge, containing 'a cooper, a cobbler, a wheelwright and cabinet maker, a blacksmith, a hatter, two physicians, a tavern, a carding machine for wool, two stores and two saloons'. The young Lincoln slept in a room behind the store, joining in the rough and tumble of a life whose sports were square dancing, wolf hunts, wrestling and gander pulling.[7] At the same time he used his leisure hours for self-instruction, reading mathematics and English literature and joining the New Salem Debating Society.

His neighbours liked this tall, awkward, gangling young

---

[6] Frank Thistlethwaite, *The Great Experiment*, p. 111.
[7] A gander was hung down from a branch of a tree and a rider riding at full speed tried to snap its head off.

man who had bested the champion wrestler and had shown a talent for thoughtful humorous talk. In 1832 Lincoln was emboldened to stand for the local state legislature—an ambitious move but one offering an avenue of quick success in frontier society. His campaign was interrupted by Black Hawk, the Leader of the Sauks and Foxes, crossing into Illinois with 500 Indian warriors. The call went out for volunteers and Lincoln joined them, being elected captain of the New Salem company. His eighty days' service did not bring him any actual warfare but provided both a new experience and a wider range of Illinois friends.

He returned to be beaten in his political campaign though he had the satisfaction of winning 277 of the 300 votes in New Salem. Moreover, he had served his apprenticeship in the art of frontier politics, travelling through the countryside to talk to farmers, making stirring speeches to loungers at county stores and using his fist to deal with an obstreperous heckler. At the same time he found himself out of a job as his patron decided to sell out. The opportunity soon arose of going into partnership with another storekeeper and Lincoln took it. A store of his own was a great thing, and a storekeeper on the frontier was a position of importance, for he presided over 'a focus of community life, a political forum and a social club, where loungers whiled away the empty hours, clustered about the stove in winter or on the porch in summer, a place to meet friends and exchange news and gossip'. But the partnership was not a success and Lincoln ended up deeply in debt. Gratefully he accepted the position of postmaster at New Salem, augmenting the meagre remuneration of fifty-five dollars per annum by turning his hand to anything that offered, from splitting rails to surveying new land.

He was rescued from this typical frontier life of a 'Jack of all trades' by his political ambition. In 1834 he stood again as a candidate for the state legislature with the backing of the local Whig leader, John T. Stuart. It was Stuart who encouraged him to study law, a subject which had always attracted Lincoln and which the comparative leisure of the post office made possible. Working on his own, he mastered Blackstone's *Commentaries* and Chitty's *Pleadings*, both bought at a local auction. By September 1836 he was called to the bar and given licence to practise. By then he had served for two years in the state legislature, impressing his Whig colleagues with his honesty and native political ability. His humble origins were no barrier to advancement in a frontier community and by 1838 he was accepted as a coming young man in Springfield, the new capital of Illinois, where he had established a law office in partnership with Stuart. From this office he looked out on the half-finished town, its streets deep in mud with hogs roaming at large. The half-finished State house reared its classical columns as a challenge that this frontier capital was merely at the beginning of a great future. And it was from this office that he went out to practise law on circuit, travelling by horse over the open prairies from one county town to another. Harsh weather, crowded accommodation and long journeys did not diminish the excitement of the circuit. When the judge was in town it was a gala week and everyone flocked to be there. It was this rough, boisterous, friendly life which provided Lincoln with his fund of humorous stories but, more important, it deepened his knowledge of the ordinary people from which he himself had sprung. With his eye always on politics, he saw the grass roots of democracy at ground level. On many evenings in rough-hewn cabins he heard arguments on local and national issues conducted in a spirit of sound common sense; every man had the right for his opinion to be heard, just as every man had to be prepared to do any job in a world where experts were few. Though Lincoln quickly became a leader and though he himself appears from his periodic melancholia to have been conscious of something unusual in himself, he never lost touch with the frontier. 'He would grow beyond his old associates but not away from them.'[8]

In the frontier, then, Lincoln was born and bred. By itself, this does not explain him, for as he himself said, 'your own resolution to succeed is more important than any other thing'. It was this resolution which prevented him from becoming merely a hired hand, a saloon lounger or a small-town lawyer. However, the frontier conditioned him as it did millions of

[8] This and other quotations in this sketch of Lincoln's early life come from B. P. Thomas, *Abraham Lincoln*.

other Americans in the 19th century. The easy-going, humorous, egalitarian life, which was based on the harsh realities of toil, became transfigured in the person of this huge, awkward man with the massive hands and rebellious hair. Described as the 'original gorilla' when he went to Washington in 1861, he personified many frontier qualities together with a compassionate humanity all his own. Much more than Andrew Jackson, the hot-tempered general from Tennessee, Lincoln represented the frontier.

The immediate effect of the frontier on politics was to create the Jacksonian Democratic party[9] which canalized the rough-and-tumble of frontier politics, where every man was as good as his neighbour and where every man could do any job, including a political one, as well as his neighbour. In this individualist society, loyalties were usually local ones, and the Democratic success of Jackson and his successor Van Buren lasted only as long as did the local desire to destroy the power of the eastern seaboard; a desire found in the Westerner who objected to restraints on his unfettered freedom to move westwards[10]; in the Southern planter who disliked the exploitation of the South by Northern tariffs, and in the labourer of the North-East who was opposed to the power of Northern capitalists. Once these desires had been partly satisfied, the Jacksonian coalition broke up and the Whig party was able to win the election of 1840.

By local interests we do not simply mean the interests of parish, town or city. In America there is a unique political group known as the section. To understand this best, let us look at Europe. Certain areas there have common interests which do not coincide with political frontiers; for example,

[9] The origins of Jacksonian Democracy are, however, extremely complex. A. M. Schlesinger, Jr. discusses them in his *Age of Jackson* and emphasizes the important part played by the industrial workers of the North-East.

[10] In 1829, for example, a senator from Connecticut proposed that the sale of Western lands should be restricted. Eastern politicians in general were anxious to keep the price of land high (Compare the problems in 19th-century Australia and the land proposals of Gibbon Wakefield.)

e lands along the Danube or the Rhine, or the lands now
ontained in the European Economic Union. Until recently the
olitical divisions of Europe have been so rigid that these areas
ith common interests have usually been unable to act to-
ether for their common purpose. In America there have al-
ays been similar areas; in colonial days, New England was
rimarily concerned with trade while the Southern colonies of
irginia, North and South Carolina and Georgia were con-
erned with planting tobacco, rice and cotton. With the ex-
ansion westwards a division arose between the old communi-
es of the Eastern seaboard and the new communities in the
est. When the Mississippi Valley was settled, inhabitants in
e older states in the North and South had a common interest
the great river which was the main artery of trade and com-
unication. When railways and canals provided an alternative
eans of communication, the North-West developed a differ-
t interest from the South-West of the valley, which con-
ued to depend on the Mississippi River. Americans have
lled these areas of common interest *sections* and, in the
merican West where the political unit, the state, was of re-
nt origin, it was the section rather than the state which
spired political action. In Europe, by contrast, it has been
e national state which has usually overshadowed any Eu-
pean sectional interest.

Sectionalism as a force in American history is an extremely
owerful one. Sections are of all kinds and are not simply geo-
aphical areas; climate, racial origins of the people and the
fferent economic activities of the inhabitants are all measures
sectional distinction. A state may align itself with other
ates for some particular interest (for example, the provision
electric power from the rivers of the Far West) and yet
ay change its alignment on some other issue—for example,
hether the American tariff should remain at its present level
not. States with a large Catholic population will line up with
ch other on a religious issue while they may be opposed to
ch other on an economic issue. There has always been this
nflict of interests in the United States, between one section
d another. A section comes together to fight at the political
vel in the houses of Congress to achieve its common purpose.

Bargains and compromises will be entered into with other sections; there is give and take between the different interests. If the way in which senators and representatives of the various states vote is examined, it can be seen how on different issues they vote with different allies. Political parties are subject to sectional pressures, and members of Congress usually feel a stronger loyalty to their section than to their party. They know that they are sent to Washington to represent the interests of their state and section and that, if they fail to do so, they will not be re-elected. They come as sectional ambassadors rather than as national representatives.

Conflict between sectional interests is therefore a natural and healthy feature of the American political system. Except for the Civil War crisis, compromise has always been reached on any issue important enough to threaten the disruption of the Union. In the making of the constitution, compromise was reached to protect the interests of the large and small states (the clause allowing each state irrespective of size two senators) and those of the slave-owning states (the clause allowing slaves to count as three-fifths in the allotment of representatives). The crisis of 1798 arose when the Federalist party whose stronghold was New England, used its control of the Federal government to pass the Alien and Sedition Acts. These Acts, aimed against the pro-French Democratic party, provoked the famous Kentucky and Virginia resolutions in which these two states declared the Acts to be unconstitutional. The collapse of the Federalist party in the elections of 1800 ended the crisis. In 1814 the New England states felt so aggrieved by the policies of Jefferson and Madison, which had resulted in the War of 1812 with England, that they gathered in convention at Hartford in 1814 to decide on steps to amend the constitution. The victory of New Orleans and the ending of the war silenced this sectional protest and in the succeeding ten years—the era of good feelings—all states co-operated in the revival of commerce after the war and in the expansion to the West. This era showed the power of national interest over sectional interest. But inevitably a new sectional pattern soon arose, as industry in the North-East and a purely cotton economy in the South made the interests of these sections diverge increasingly. The South increased its cotton crop enormously to meet the demands of the English textile market.[11] It was able to do this because of the cotton gin invented by Eli Whitney. The English market and the ease of cotton production discouraged the growth of Southern industry and very soon the South resented the high tariff imposed in the interests of North-Eastern manufacturers. The crisis came with the so-called 'Tariff of Abominations' in 1828, which provoked South Carolina's theory of Nullification. This theory, elaborated by John C. Calhoun, claimed that a state had the right to nullify a Federal law, and if necessary to secede from the Union. Here was an echo of 1798. In 1832 South Carolina passed a Nullification Ordinance which made President Jackson threaten to use Federal forces to enforce the law. Only a compromise tariff bill proposed by Henry Clay of Kentucky resolved a crisis which might well have led to bloodshed.

In all these crises, 1798, 1814 and 1832, sectional interests were thought to be threatened but in each one the weapon used was the cry of 'states' rights'.[12] This doctrine claimed that, since the union was a compact between sovereign states, the states were of more importance than the Union and that each state had the right to protect its own interests. It was a nice legalistic point, but it only had practical significance when a section needed a constitutional argument to defend its position. A civil war was required to kill the states' rights argument and to assert, once and for all, that the American Union, though created by sovereign states, became after its creation something greater than the states comprising it.

These three famous crises were merely like the top of the iceberg of American sectionalism. They showed the tension of the American Union at its most extreme, and to concentrate on them is to ignore the many healthy examples of sectional interests being reconciled. Henry Clay, the author of the tariff compromise in 1833, was fully aware of the need to satisfy

[11] 171,000 bales in 1810; 731,000 bales in 1830; 2,133,000 bales in 1850; 5,387,000 bales in 1859.

[12] The recent (1957) action of Governor Faubus in Arkansas has echoed the states' rights argument but it is really only of significance if Arkansas represents the South as a section on the issue of Negro segregation. Whether she does so is not at all certain.

sectional rivalries. He proposed his famous 'American System' by which tariffs would both satisfy the industrial manufacturers and, at the same time, provide funds to establish a transport system in the West and to improve the navigation of Southern rivers. Besides this, he hoped that Southern cotton would find a market in Northern textile mills. Unfortunately this 'system' did not go far enough. The complexities of the sectional pattern and the rapid development of America in population, territory and ideas meant that the 'American System' did not begin to satisfy the sectional interests of the South. To understand this we must now look at this development.

Until about 1830 the West, although it had a sectional character of its own, had had extremely close links with the South. Emigration westwards had come from Virginia into Kentucky, along the Cumberland Pike and into the river valleys which finally reached the Mississippi. The settlers in Ohio, Indiana and Illinois were as closely linked in one way with the Old South as were those who populated the new states of Alabama, Mississippi and Louisiana. Trade depended on river communication and New Orleans was the outlet of a trading system which reached to the farthest backwoods settlement in Ohio. Western corn, bacon, whisky and tobacco were brought to the country store on the river bank and, while the farmer collected his new supplies (which had been brought by paddle steamer from New Orleans up the Mississippi), he learnt all the political news and local gossip at the counter. This connection of South and West was not simply economic; the preachers who brought religion, the politicians who stumped the wilderness and the new settlers, all had roots in the Old South rather than in the North-East. The first stage of westward expansion was a Southern movement and the alliance of South and West was a major factor in politics. The change came in the 1830's. Already the cotton boom had led a new type of emigrant to the rich lands of Mississippi and Alabama. Penniless planting families from the Carolina seaboard sent overseers or younger sons to establish plantations. They were followed by ruthless and ambitious men who knew that they could wrest a fortune from the land by recklessly exploiting its richness, using gangs of slave labour. This movement to the

outh-West created the new cotton kingdom which pushed its
oundaries into Texas and inspired the aggression against
Mexico in the 1840's. It was a new type of Western frontier,
eopled by sons of the old seaboard South giving new life to
avery and re-creating an appearance of an old and gracious
lantation life. It had little in common with the earlier South-
n movement to the West, to Ohio and Missouri where the
mall farmer toiled to produce a mixed crop with little slave
bour. The New South-West was based on cotton and slavery.

The second change in the West came from the North-East
nd was caused by a revolution in transport. In 1825 the Erie
anal was opened which linked New York with Lake Erie.
ther canals in the years which followed soon provided a sys-
m of communications allowing the trade of the North-West
 flow eastwards. Canals were rapidly supplemented by rail-
ays which were at first built to widen the area served by a
wn like Buffalo or Cleveland. Though the financial panic of
837 interrupted this development, by 1840 the North-West
as already sprouting railway lines to the East while the
altimore and Ohio Railroad had opened the first passenger
rvice. By 1853 a continuous line joined New York and Chi-
go. Between 1840 and 1860 28,000 miles were added to the
isting 3,300, the bulk of the mileage being built in the North
d West. In 1817 it took an average of 52 days to transport
ods by river and wagon from the Ohio River to Philadelphia;
 1850 it took 6–8 days by rail. Not only did the railways
vert a considerable quantity of Western trade from the
uth to the North-East,[18] but they made possible a new and
latively easier flow of migration to the area of the Great
kes. Upper state New York became the starting point for
migration which peopled Michigan, Wisconsin, Iowa and
innesota and which increased the populations of Ohio, In-
ana and Illinois with men whose memories lay in the North-
st or in Europe. Immigration from Europe had begun to
crease after 1830 with the peak in the pre-Civil War period
ing reached in 1854 with the figure of 427,000. The bulk

[18] Although down to 1860 the turnover of trade at New Orleans
ntinued to increase, it was largely made up of the increased cot-
n production of the South-West.

of the immigrants were either Irish, Scandinavian or German
The Irish generally remained in the cities since they were with
out even the small resources needed to leave them.[14] The
became the unskilled labour for the new canals, factories an
railways. Many of the two remaining groups went to the West
Most of them were peasants and they tried to make their wa
West, by canal or railway, to the regions already partly set
tled by their own racial groups.[15] If they landed at a Souther
port they could travel cheaply by the river system to the Mi
sissippi. There was little attraction to remain in the Sout
which provided small opportunity for the poor white an
where yellow fever and cholera took a heavy toll. Skilled im
migrants found a ready demand for their labour in the infan
industries of the North-East and the contribution they mad
to American industrial expansion cannot be overrated.

These developments from 1830 onwards made the section
pattern much more complicated. The old alliance of the tw
agrarian sections—the South and the West—slowly gave wa
before an alliance of North-West and North-East against th
Old South and the South-West. Immigration, railways, indu
try and trade steadily transformed the character of the Nort
in both the East and the West, while the South, both the Ol
and the New, remained relatively stationary in population an
dependent on the cotton crop for her economy.

It has been well said that

> By 1850 a greater North and a greater South had
> emerged as two distinct cultures within the American Un-
> ion, the one democratic, capitalistic, ambitious and mor-
> ally cocksure, growing fast in people and empire, and
> on the threshold of industrialism; the other lagging in
> growth, agrarian, tradition-minded, caste conscious and
> proud; the one representing a new modern world coming
> into being, the other an older order destined to be over-
> whelmed.

Henry Clay's 'American System' was designed for a differe

---

[14] Boston and New York today have a very large Irish populatic
[15] Scandinavians in Minnesota, Germans in Wisconsin and M
souri.

state of affairs from this; it could hope to reconcile different sectional interests but not those of two different civilizations. Sectionalism was healthy when the lines of sectional distinction were not rigidly drawn. The emergence of a greater North and a greater South tragically over-simplified the sectional conflict in the United States. A wide variety of different interests became divided simply on the issue of slavery. On this issue two great sections came into being.

CHAPTER III

SLAVERY AND ABOLITION

Industry, immigration and railways, or the lack of them, had much to do with the growth of these two great sections. But it was the ideas which came out of these conditions which proved the governing factor in dividing the North and the South. Of course, all men in the North and South did not think in one way: the vast majority of men often do not think consistently at all. It is politicians, journalists and pamphleteers who attribute to a group the ideas of an individual. Jealousy had always existed between sections in America and this jealousy led the public men of each section to construct a stereotyped picture of their sectional rivals. As early as 1834 the English visitor Harriet Martineau, one of the most famous 19th-century bluestockings, remarked:

> Hatred is not too strong a term for this sectional prejudice. Many a time in America have I been conscious of that pang and shudder which are felt only in the presence of hatred . . . I have scarcely known whether to laugh or to mourn when I have been told that the New England people are all pedlars or canting priests, that the people of the South are all heathens and those of the West all barbarians. Trifling as some instances appear of the manifestation of this puerile spirit, it sometimes, it always issues in results which are no trifle—always because the spirit of jealousy is a deadly curse to him who is possessed by it, whether it be founded on fact or no.

In the years after Miss Martineau had written, moral passion was added to jealousy, and the result was that the sections lost sight of the mutual usefulness that might result from their differences and instead began to emphasize points of difference as points of incompatibility.

It was slavery and the abolitionist attack upon it which injected moral passion into the sectional conflict. Although the majority of Americans would have preferred to ignore this issue, it ultimately became the all-important mark of sectional differences. Slavery had existed in America since the settlement of Virginia in the early 17th century, but by the time of the American revolution men expected it to die out within a generation. Not only was the need for slave labour dying out as the tobacco and indigo crops declined in the seaboard South, but Americans also felt the influence of the anti-slavery sentiment which gained enormous strength in England during the last decade of the 18th century. The constitution certainly protected existing slaves, but Article I, Section 9, envisaged the ending of the slave trade by 1808. A number of enlightened planters followed Jefferson's example and freed their slaves in their wills. Then came the invention in 1793 of Eli Whitney's cotton gin which enabled the cotton seed to be easily separated from the lint. Within a generation this invention, together with the demand from Lancashire, revitalized the declining agrarian economy of the South. In cotton lay an easy crop to grow in the rich virgin lands of the Mississippi basin; the labour force already existed in the slaves who could endure the heavy work in a hot climate. It was small wonder that Southerners gave up the plans they had had in the early years of the century of using their capital to promote industry in the South. Cotton involved less risk and immediate profits, so any surplus capital was quickly sunk in more slaves and the purchase of new cotton lands in the West. The acceptable time for change had passed.

Thus the South turned its back on both the infant industries of the North-East and on its former willingness to see the gradual extinction of slavery. Slaves were required in increasing numbers as expansion drove into the South-West. From a million in 1800 the total number increased to nearly 4½ million in 1860. After 1808, the overseas slave trade was forbidden by Congress but smuggling continued to a limited degree, and the old seaboard states, particularly Virginia and Maryland, became in course of time a market for an internal slave trade to channel Negroes to the cotton areas of the Mississippi and the South-West. The South became a section dependent on a one-crop economy and saddled with the intractable problem of the Negro. Moreover, the rewards did not last for long. The rosy dreams of riches gained from cotton were quickly scattered as over-production brought a fall in prices. In the 1820's the average price was 15 cents a lb.; by the 1850's it had sunk to 9 cents. The price of slaves, on the contrary, rose with the demand from 350 dollars in 1800 to over 1500 dollars in 1860 for a field hand in first-class condition. Dependent on a world market for their cotton prices, there was nothing the Southern planter could do to force Lancashire to raise the level. A bad year could mean debt for a planter, and before long, most cotton planters were in debt to Northern merchants who advanced money and supplies on the credit of the next year's crop. Observers of Southern plantations[1] have usually commented on the lack of amenities which contrasted with the lavish hospitality. Plantation houses differed widely between a mansion, sixty-five feet square, two stories high, both verandaed' to a one-horse cotton plantation described by Mark Twain:

A rail fence round a two acre yard . . . big double log house for the white folk, and hewed logs with the chinks stopped up with mud and mortar and these mud stripes been whitewashed sometime or another . . . three little log nigger cabins in a row t'other side the smoke ouse . . . bench by the kitchen door with a bucket of water and a gourd; hound asleep there in the sun; more hounds asleep roundabout, about three shade trees off in a corner; some currant bushes and gooseberry bushes in one place by the fence and outside the fence a garden and a water melon patch; then the cotton fields begin.

[1] W. H. Russell, the famous *Times* correspondent, kept a most interesting diary about his visit to America in 1861–62. It has recently been republished as *My Civil War Diary*. His observations in the South are particularly revealing.

Whatever the status of the plantation, debt was a constant guest.

The South's failure to diversify its economy and its reliance on a single crop placed it in a desperate position. Logically there were only two courses open to it: either to develop industries and a variety of crops, or to continue to expand since the cotton lands in the West were quickly exhausted by wasteful methods. Some Southern leaders attempted to encourage interest in industry but, although there was a lot of talk, there was insufficient capital available to sink in mills and railways. Moreover, the Southerner, whether white or Negro, did not take easily to the idea of industry, and European immigrants did not relish settling in a slave society. To continue as before or to support extravagant ideas of expansion seemed the most natural course to follow.

Inevitably there was jealousy of the North. Merchants in New York were the middle men who appeared to bleed the South of all its profits, not only by selling them Northern manufactured goods but also by charging high commissions and freight charges for handling the cotton crop. This resentment led to a disparagement of Northern society and its way of life, so rapidly changing from the 1830's onwards as increasing population and early industrialization transformed its character. Of course, both the North-East and the North-West were still predominantly agricultural but even here the contrast with the South was enormous. A diversified economy with wheat, bacon, beef and dairy products produced a richer and more stable society. Through jealousy, Southerners were driven to exalt their own society, to place on a pedestal the ideal of the Southern gentleman, courteous to women and quick on the draw, of the graceful plantation life and its scale of values which claimed to be cultured and aristocratic in contrast to the grasping commercial and democratic values of the Yankee North. This picture of themselves ignored many realities: the 'poor whites' despised by black and white living in poverty and disease in the barren uplands of Georgia or Mississippi, the brutal exploitation of the slave gangs in the South-West, well removed from the elegances of the seaboard, the lack of a public educational or library system. Nevertheless

his Southern picture of themselves had sufficient truth to en-
ist the finest talent of the South in its defence in Congress.
'or generations, Southern politicians used their influence at
Washington for the sole purpose of protecting the South in its
osing fight as a minority in the nation. The real tragedy was
hat the fact of slavery, the South's 'peculiar institution', so
ound all Southerners together, that no Southerner was ever
ble to be really revolutionary and suggest a solution to the
'outh's situation which became more desperate every year.

To the Southerner slavery was to be looked at in three ways,
ocially, economically and morally. It was the last of these
vays which was paramount to abolitionists, but to Southern-
rs, whether of the Old South or of the New South-West,
heir 'peculiar institution' could not be viewed so simply.
Vhether slavery was morally wrong or economically doomed,
he existence of the Negro in their midst affected every South-
rner. At a generous estimate only 350,000 men in the South
eld slaves and of these only 46,000 owned more than twenty.
'et 8 million Southerners defended slavery because, though
hey may have had no pecuniary interest in slavery, 'they have
social interest at stake that is worth more to them than all
he wealth of the Indies'. Even Hinton R. Helper, who at-
acked slavery economically from the point of view of the non-
lave-holder in his book *The Impending Crisis* (1857), loathed
ie Negro and had no wish that the South should be other
ian a white man's country. This was the view of all the South-
rn whites, the majority of whom were yeoman farmers who
aised corn, hogs and a little cotton or tobacco along the Ap-
alachian slopes to the fringes of the black belt.

It was this social aspect of slavery which made any easy
olution difficult. In the 1820's many thoughtful Southerners
ad talked openly and frankly about the possibility of abolish-
g the institution, and many had subscribed to Colonization
ocieties to send the Negro back to Africa. But the increasing
emand for labour in the cotton fields and the beginning of
nti-slavery attacks from Northerners silenced this liberal opin-
n. With the increasing violence of abolitionist attacks, con-
entrating simply on the moral issue, Southerners began to
efend their 'peculiar institution'. They became increasingly

sensitive on the subject; the newspapers gave widespread publicity to abolitionist propaganda by printing it in order to denounce it. Already they were conscious of falling behind the North in power and resources; they were conscious, too, of the nationalist tendency within the framework of the Federal system to overpower the rights of minorities. These fears focused on slavery, once that institution was attacked. At first they sought to palliate the institution and to deny its failings: in the end they gloried in it, claiming that it was biblically ordained, that it produced the most civilized of societies and that it was a positive good. From there they went on to the attack, denouncing Northern society with its grossness, its vulgarity, its slums and its labour troubles. To us with the advantage of hindsight, nothing could be more pathetic or tragic than that Jefferson Davis, future President of the Confederacy, could declare in 1859, 'there is probably not an intelligent mind among our own citizens who doubts either the moral or the legal right of the institution of African slavery'. In 1859 slavery existed only in Cuba, Puerto Rico, Dutch Guiana and Brazil, in most of which there also existed a large half-breed population to act as a bridge between the races. While the whole of the civilized world was moving in one direction, the South was moving in another. Even if the South had won her independence in the Civil War she would still have had to face the civilized world on this issue.

Except then for a short period Southerners never faced the issue of slavery squarely; and before very long it became a symbol of their whole minority status within the Union. They defended slavery irrespective of its character. In the Old South the traditional form of slavery has been called feudal slavery. Here the centre was the plantation where the slave lived under a type of serfdom, in a hut of his own with opportunities for a family life and a certain amount of education. If he were a house servant he became very much a part of the household. This feudal slavery was on the whole kindly and sincere, and many planters thought of it as a means by which the Negro could eventually be trained for a qualified liberty. Benevolent and paternal, the best slave-owner treated his slaves as children, using the rod only if required. As one old slave recalled after the Civil War was over: 'Old Master done showed me how to git along in this world. I just go up and ask him what he want me to do and he'll tell me and iffen I don't know how, he'll show me how and I'll try to do it to please him. And when I get it done, I wants to hear him grumble like he used to and say "Charley you ain't got no sense but you is a good boy!"' Within this system the slaves, with inevitable exceptions, led a contented life, fed, clothed and housed and partaking of the social activities of the plantation community. For the good master realized that a happy plantation paid dividends in discipline and hard work. But to achieve this required a busy life, both for him and his wife who looked after the children and womenfolk. Where an overseer was left in charge, conditions might be very different; against a cruel and corrupt white man the slave had no defence. Yet even in the happiest plantation a hidden fear of the black man in their midst always lay beneath the surface. The slave insurrection in Southampton County, Virginia, in 1831 when 57 whites were killed underlined this fear, and throughout the South slave codes were strengthened, making the black man no more than a chattel.

This feudal slavery was not transported to the cotton fields of the South-West. Here commercial slavery developed, with slaves organized in gangs and ruthlessly driven to exploit the land. It was from this form of slavery that the abolitionists drew most of their illustrations and Simon Legree in *Uncle Tom's Cabin* (ironically a New Englander) is the example of the brutal white man at his worst. Obviously conditions were not uniform but in the frontier South, where slaves had been recently purchased, there would be little humanitarian restraint. Just as industrialists in New England factories exploited their labour to produce profits, so did the plantation-owner, desperately seeking to win a larger cotton crop from the land. The difference was in the absolute power that the planter had over the slave. Linked with this commercial slavery was the internal slave trade. This traffic in human beings was the most deplorable side of slavery; families were split, auctions were held in most towns and advertisements appeared in every paper. The slaver became a feature of American life and his ap-

pearance in Northern cities to recover fugitive slaves was grist
to the abolitionist mill.

It was the growth of intense anti-slavery sentiment in that
part of the nation where factories and great merchants were
concentrated which tragically over-simplified the problem of
slavery, making no distinction between the types and failing
to regard it as a social and economic problem as well as a
moral one. The extent of industrialization in the North-East
must not be overstated. It was only in 1859 that the value of
the products of American industry exceeded for the first time
the value of agricultural products. The previous ten years had
seen an enormous expansion due mainly to the great advance
in transport. In the decade before the Civil War railway mileage trebled, the merchant marine outdistanced that of Great
Britain and the Mississippi and Niagara were bridged. Before
1850 machinery had been adapted to the use of many industries and after 1850 steam power was generally introduced.
Until then water power had usually served. The New England
textile industry had grown from using 2,000 spindles in 1800
to 2,280,000 in 1850 and 5,235,000 in 1860. Small wonder
that Lowell, Massachusetts, was known as the Manchester of
America. Eli Whitney had introduced the principle of stand-
ardized parts and by 1850 the iron industry, which had developed slowly, was producing a swelling flood of ploughs,
stoves, reapers, pistols and harvesters. The McCormick factory
had opened in Chicago in 1847. Factories remained small,
however; typical were those of Connecticut producing Colt
revolvers and Winchester rifles. A rapidly increasing population provided a growing home market. It was this market that
Northern industry served, whereas the South, with her cotton,
provided over half the exports of the United States. New York
and New Orleans shared the primacy for commerce, but New
Orleans relied increasingly on the trade in cotton whereas over
70 per cent of the import trade flowed through New York.

By 1850 then it would be true to say that America had
begun that phenomenal industrial expansion which the Civil
War was to stimulate. This industrialization was mainly concentrated in the greater North; the following table shows very

clearly how far one can talk of an industrial North compared
with an agrarian South:

MANUFACTURES IN 1860

Section	No. of factories*	Capital invested	Average no. of labourers	Annual value of products
		$		$
New England	20,671	257,478,000	391,846	468,599,000
Middle States	53,387	435,062,000	546,240	802,338,000
Western States	36,785	194,213,000	209,900	384,607,000
Southern States	20,631	95,976,000	110,720	155,531,000

* 'Factory' covers any unit, however small. The important figure is the
capital invested in industrial units.

Obviously the bulk of labour was still concerned with agri-
culture. In the thirty years before 1860 agricultural production
had been steadily moving westwards. New York and Pennsylvania, once the foremost wheat producers, gave way to
Ohio, Illinois, Indiana and Wisconsin; in corn and the hogs
which ate it, Kentucky, Tennessee and Virginia gave way to
Illinois, Ohio and Indiana. New York and Pennsylvania became leading industrial and trading states; Kentucky and Tennessee had a sufficiently varied agricultural economy to pros-
per whereas Virginia stagnated. The agricultural North-West,
with its continually expanding production, had a market in
the North-East; the South depended on selling its cotton in a
market which was temporarily saturated by 1860. Thus factories and farms worked by white labour, a growing immigrant
population and far-flung transport links between North-East
and North-West gave to the greater North a character of its
own. Cincinnati, Cleveland, Buffalo, Pittsburgh and an infant
Chicago were centres, at first for their own vicinity and eventually for a Northern network of trade, industry and agricul-
ture with strong connections through New York and Boston
with Europe.

Even more than economic differences, the most vivid contrast with the South was the vitality of the North's life in
education, literature and radical ideas. For the North was not
isolated from the flow of European ideas, many of which were
quickened by the impact of the Western frontier. Words like

Democracy and Liberty, so compelling to the Liberal of 19th-century Europe, took on new life when transferred to America. In the years after 1815 religious, democratic and humanitarian movements swept through New England and the major Northern cities. A traffic in ideas took place across the Atlantic. Radicals like Francis Place, idealists like Robert Owen and the evangelical energy of Quakers, Baptists and Unitarians stimulated demands for political and social reform. America, 'the world's best hope', appeared to provide an environment where progress would not be killed by the dead hand of the past. Inevitably these demands brought in their wake fads and eccentricities[2] which may cause amused comment but cannot hide the powerful forces which were changing the moral and intellectual temper of the age. This transatlantic ferment produced schemes of Utopian socialism, progressive education, new ideas of diet and physical culture. These had little effect, in contrast to the campaigns for temperance, women's rights and improved conditions for the insane and for convicts. America entered the field of reform with extravagance and unquenchable optimism.

New England produced Thoreau and Emerson, the philosophers of individualism, who exhorted Americans to soar to the heights that human nature was capable of reaching; who told them that 'in every age of the world there has been a leading nation, one of a more generous sentiment whose eminent citizens were willing to stand for the interests of general justice and humanity'. Walt Whitman, the poet of democracy, taught that America had the great destiny of showing the world how to live democratically. This spirit of good will and hope encouraged the belief that the preamble to the Declaration of Independence could be made a reality. It also stimulated movements for humanitarian and social reform whose inspiration was primarily religious. The nearest comparison is with the religious volcano which burst over England in the 1650's

---

[2] A general convention was held in Boston in 1840 where 'madmen, madwomen, men with beards, Dunkers, Muggletonians, Come Outers, Groaners, Agrarians, Seventh Day Adventists, Baptists, Quakers, Abolitionists, Calvinists, Unitarians and philosophers, all came successively to the top and seized their moment, if not their hour, wherein to chide or pray or preach or protest'.

when Calvinism sought to establish the reign of God on earth. Fifth Monarchy men, Levellers and Quakers were no longer satisfied with Calvinist salvation; they had to be up and doing as Christians in the past had done at times of revival. Dorothea Dix and her fight for the insane, Elizabeth Cady Stanton and her crusade for women's rights, Theodore Dwight Weld and William Lloyd Garrison, the spokesmen of slavery abolition, are examples of the spirit which was to transform America. Nor should John B. Gough be forgotten who declared, 'While I can talk against drink, I'll talk; when I can only whisper I'll do that; and when I cannot whisper any longer, faith I'll make motions—they say I'm good at that'.

The focus of the revival was in New England and the Greek towns of Upper State New York. Here originated the Millerites, followers of William Miller who proclaimed that 1843 would see the end of the world. 1843 came and went; the new date, October 22nd, 1844, saw thousands of people assembled in tents outside towns to wait in torrential rain for a climax which never came. Here also lived the Fox sisters, the famous spirit rappers, and most important of all Joseph Smith, the young man of Palmyra, who founded the Mormon sect when a vision revealed to him the hiding place of the golden plates on which were engraved the history of the lost tribes of Israel. This 'book of Mormon' was 'sealed by the hand of the prophet Moroni and hid up unto the Lord to come forth in due time by way of the Gentile'. But these were extravagancies in a period of profound religious revival. The leaders of the anti-slavery movement underwent religious conversion in a more normal way, just as in England leaders of the movement like William Wilberforce and Zachary Macaulay had done. Between 1824 and 1842 Charles G. Finney, the most famous of all revivalist preachers, conducted a series of triumphant revivals in the middle and eastern states. At one of them, in Utica, New York, he converted, after a hard struggle, Theodore Weld, who became one of the most important figures in the anti-slavery cause—'eloquent as an angel and powerful as thunder'.

It is obvious that in a period of religious revival and reform movements, slavery would provide a dissonance too harsh to be borne; and it rapidly became a target for reforming activity.

The same men who led movements against alcoholism and prison conditions championed the cause of slavery abolition. Weld became a powerful force converting some of the people who were to be most enthusiastic agents for abolition. Harriet Beecher Stowe, Joshua Giddings, the leader of the anti-slavery forces in Congress, James G. Birney, one-time planter in Alabama and the presidential candidate of the Liberty party in 1840, Edwin M. Stanton, Lincoln's Secretary of War—all were brought to abolitionism through Weld. Besides these prominent names there were dozens of local agents.

The anti-slavery movement had three phases. In 1817 the American Colonization Society had been established with the purpose of shipping the Negro back to Africa. This object had support from all sections and there was nothing necessarily humanitarian in it. The desire was to get rid of a degraded element in American society. But the task was a formidable one; in all, between 1820 and 1866, only 11,090 Negroes were sent back to Africa. It is interesting to see that Lincoln in 1858 said, 'My first impulse would be to free all slaves and send them to Liberia', yet as this was impossible, 'if all earthly powers were given to me I should not know what to do, as to the existing institution'. But if Lincoln did not know in 1858 others, as early as 1830, were quite clear. Slavery was a sin and must be abolished. This must be done at once without compensation and the freed slaves must have the full rights of free men granted to them. The overshadowing of the Colonization Society—the one national attempt to deal with the problem—by those who held that slavery was a sin is marked by the foundation of the American Anti-Slavery Society in 1833. This grew out of the union of the New England Society, founded the previous year by William Lloyd Garrison, and a group in New York led by the merchant Lewis Tappan. Garrison, the most violent and unsympathetic of all the agitators, had already started a paper called *The Liberator*. He was a man on the border-line of madness and he did much to bring ridicule on the anti-slavery movement by the extravagancies of his other reforming schemes. In 1840 the other abolitionists broke with Garrison, who continued his own wild way, issuing every week the most vindictive and bitter editorials in his paper and advocating the secession of the North.

The third phase opened in 1839 when Weld, who had virtually taken command of the movement, decided that the anti-slavery forces should enter the political field. The Liberty party was formed and it contested the presidency. Politically the abolitionists had no success, in 1840 gaining 7,059 votes, in 1844 62,300. The Free Soil party of 1848 won only 291,000 votes in a total poll of 2¼ million and in 1852 the Free Democrats received 156,000. The numbers in the abolition societies spread across the Northern and Western states were small and the circulation of *The Liberator* was minute.[3] Yet their success in other fields was enormous, for effects cannot necessarily be judged by statistics. The existence of a group of men and women who worried the slavery question like a bone was an enormous influence. They petitioned Congress[4]; they organized the underground railroad to assist fugitive slaves; they collected facts in books like Weld's *American Slavery as it is; the testimony of a 1000 witnesses,* on which *Uncle Tom's Cabin* was based; and they had their martyrs in men like Elijah Lovejoy, an anti-slavery editor killed by an incensed mob in Illinois in 1837. Above all, they had in the pulpits of a thousand churches a platform from which to proclaim consistently the fundamental sin of slavery. They refused to allow people to shirk the issue, to comfort themselves with rationalizations for the lazy intellect and sedatives for the guilty conscience. They would not be silent and they would not equivocate. They broke the conspiracy of silence which everyone, particularly the politicians, would have preferred to preserve. The bulk of men like an easy way out; they feel that by muddling through they can avoid facing up to an issue. The slavery issue was one on which Northerners could very easily have turned a blind eye but for the activities of the abolitionists. The failure of the abolitionists in the political field shows that the politi-

[3] By 1836 there were 500 abolition societies; by 1840 membership was only 150,000.
[4] A 'gag' was imposed on petitions in 1836. In 1844 Congress removed it and this caused South Carolina congressmen to talk of secession for the first time.

cians were supported by the great mass of opinion in seeking
to keep slavery out of politics.

In trying to assess the reasons why a greater North and a
greater South had emerged by 1860, slavery and the abolitionist attack must take pride of place. It was the abolitionists
who, by attacking slavery, made it the symbol of the South.
Instead of being but one feature of Southern life it was made
the explanation for all parts of it. By 1860 the abolitionists
had succeeded in painting a picture of Southern slavery which
Northerners did not question. 'The thieves, the man stealers,
the whoremongers must be thrust out with headlong haste
and in holy terror that God may come in.' They had succeeded
in making a politician sensitive about his position on slavery
and in the North and East certain to declare his sentiments
against it, if only to capture votes. The avenging force of Puri-
tanism in politics was their doing and for over a generation
their representatives in Congress, Charles Sumner, Joshua P.
Giddings and Salmon P. Chase, adopted an attitude of bat-
tling for the Lord by hurling invectives and invoking divine
sanctions against opponents. As early as 1836 Finney had
warned Weld, 'Is it not true, at least do you not fear it is,
that we are in our present course going fast into a civil war?
Will not our present movements in abolition result in that?
The fact is, dear Weld, our leading abolitionists are good men,
but there are few of them wise men.' Others gave a similar
warning, but nothing could check these men armed with
righteousness.

Around the institution of slavery was engendered most of
the bitterness which made war necessary. If slavery had not
become the symbol of the South—to the North the symbol of
Southern depravity, to the South of her superiority—it might
have been faced as a national question. For the South was not
set apart from the influences at work in the East during the
1820's. In most aspects of their life Southerners were deeply at-
tached to the ideals of self-government, freedom and equality.
Admittedly their society had a stability lacking in a changing
industrial society. They had few great cities and there was,
therefore, neither the demand nor cause for many reforming
movements. But the temperance movement flourished and

schemes for prison reform were discussed. Religious revivalism also flourished but in a different way from the North; thousands gathered at camp meetings[5] in an orgy of emotion and social gaiety but they went home without any crusading spirit, for there seemed little to crusade about. If the South had been left alone Southern liberals might have faced the problem of slavery and worked out some gradual schemes of emancipation. As it was, the abolitionist demand for immediate action and the denunciation of slavery as a sin drove Southerners to defend, as a positive good, a system which preserved the South as a white man's country. With their own economic system, and increasingly conscious of falling behind the North in numbers and wealth, they became permanently aggrieved. Isolated from the forces transforming the North,[6] they saw in the abolitionist attack a dangerous threat to their whole way of life. Just as the North developed a stereotyped picture of the South as 'the Slave Power', so the South saw in the North a greedy, commercial power seeking to engulf them. Both pictures were mistaken, and both owed their origin to the abolitionist.

However much opponents of slavery attacked it as an institution, it was the moral argument which created the bitterness. Northerners claimed that slavery was economically unprofitable and that it was responsible for the backwardness of the South. The slave lacked skill, the argument ran; his status discouraged free immigration to provide the labour for industry which the South anyway could not develop as all her capital was tied up in the cost of slaves. This type of argument ignored many factors; that Southern soil was less fertile than that of other areas and that heavy rain was as responsible for soil erosion as the wastefulness of the Southern planter. Industry has only begun to appear in the South in the present cen-

[5] Well described by Mark Twain in *Huckleberry Finn*.

[6] The different development of North and South can be seen in these figures of two not untypical States. In 1836 Arkansas and Michigan were both admitted to the Union with approximately the same population.

In 1850 Arkansas had			Michigan	
"	"	162,189 whites,	"	395,071
"	"	9 newspapers	"	58
"	"	1 public library	"	280
"	"	353 schools	"	2714

tury and it is unlikely that it would have flourished in the 19th
century, even if the Negro had been free. For, by nature, the
South was a producer of raw materials, and her economic interests could well have been served by co-operation with the
North. These types of argument could have been useful and
have done much to prevent the South from feeling aggrieved.
But they could never be fruitfully discussed in the atmosphere
created by the abolitionist. The moral sword brandished by
these men lay between the two sections, dividing them irrepa-
rably by 1860. By then every issue between North and South
was coloured by slavery; every issue had become a matter of
principle, irreconcilable by compromise or natural bargaining.
It had taken thirty years for this situation to come about, for,
as we have seen, the majority of men would have preferred to
ignore the question. But the abolitionists had made this impossible; by 1860 Southern politicians were bound to react to
protect the interests of slavery whatever the cost and Northern
politicians, supported by a solid body of opinion, were determined that the extension of slavery beyond its present bounds
must be stopped. An irrepressible conflict, as it has been
called, seemed inevitable, but since human beings control their
own destinies, there was still a chance for the highest statesmanship to bridge the gulf which the extremists on both sides
had made.

CHAPTER IV

COMPROMISE AND ITS FAILURE

William Howard Russell, the English journalist, recorded in his diary for April 1st, 1861:

'I drove over to visit Senator Douglas . . . his sketch of the causes which had led to the present disruption of parties and the hazard of civil war was most vivid and able; and for more than an hour he spoke with a vigour of thought and terseness of phrase which even on such dreary and uninviting themes as squatter sovereignty and the Kansas-Nebraska question interested a foreigner in the man and the subject.'

It is these 'dreary and uninviting themes' which are the subject of this chapter; just as the history of the constitutional struggle between King and Parliament in England during the 17th century is concerned with Bates' Case, Ship Money and the Petition of Right, so the failure of compromise before the Civil War is centred on legal and constitutional matters. Over these, the two great sections whose development we have traced contested. Behind the debates in Congress, the political compromises and the legal decisions lies the reality: in the North-West the farmers of the prairies, in the North-East the factory labourer often but a year removed from his family in Europe, in Georgia the poor white scraping a living in the barren uplands. The New York docks handled a constant stream of passengers and goods in a thriving Atlantic exchange. New Orleans continued to resound with confusion of tongues and to exhibit wealth in a mixture of elegant buildings and reckless profusion among the docks. Boston, despite its Irish immigration, remained a cultural citadel where old-estab-

lished families on Beacon Hill looked askance at visitors from
the West. Everywhere, in fact, men and women pursued their
ordinary everyday lives. America was expanding and the opportunities were glittering; the gold of California (1848), the
Santa Fe trail and the semi-weekly mail service that ran between New York and San Francisco (1858) opened up a new
world. Manifest destiny beckoned both to the nation and to
the individual. All things were possible, it seemed; a man
could make a fortune with a little luck and if things turned
out wrong there was always somewhere farther West to start
anew. Politicians, journalists and preachers might thunder
warnings, but these were not the realities of life to the average
man in any part of the United States.

Southerners might abuse the 'damned Yankees' and Northerners might be excited when a fugitive slave was recaptured
in their town, but their feelings did not remain permanently
bellicose and indignant. Down to the very last moment war
was unthinkable to the vast majority. Only when the politicians failed to produce a compromise did the people fall into
line responding to sentiments which for decades had slowly
been taking root in their subconscious minds. This has been
the origin of modern wars; ordinary men and women paying
little attention to diplomatic crises and incidents and largely
ignoring the warnings of their leaders. The ordinary man has
little use for politicians, yet when politicians fail to find a way
out of a deadlock they rally to the flag to defend a way of
life which appears to be threatened. So 'the dreary and uninviting themes' which are the prelude to the coming of the
American Civil War play a larger part in history books than
they did in the lives of most people at the time. Nevertheless,
they were terribly important; for in a democratic society politicians have to talk in general terms presenting problems to the
electorate in the simplest form. This very simplicity is deceptive; the problems of sectionalism were infinitely complicated
and the issue of slavery was insuperable unless it was faced
in all its complexity. Moral indignation is a powerful weapon
in a democracy, for it welds together the conflicting hopes and
interests of different people. Thus it was that politicians in both
North and South began to use, against their better judgement,

the language of morality. Congress was less a place of national debate than a sounding box for sectional arguments. Congressmen made speeches for the consumption of their constituents; often they had their words privately printed for circulation back home. This made it difficult to go against what they had said at election time and though they were the political leaders of their state, they were, in their turn, bound by the ideas they had crystallized in the minds of the people. On many matters, of course, it was possible for Congressmen to reach a compromise by giving way on certain points, if others were maintained. But when questions were coloured by morality, compromise became difficult. 1850 saw the last great compromise on the slavery issue; the succeeding decade witnessed the failure of the politicians to maintain a compromise.

Their sectional attitudes had become fixed and they were the prisoners of these attitudes which they had done so much to create. There were many politicians of great ability, but none of them were able to overcome sectional hatreds and fears in appealing for the charity which alone could preserve the Union, 'the world's best hope'. William H. Seward of New York was deficient in tact and steadiness of judgement; Jefferson Davis of Mississippi was obstinate and lacking the common touch; Stephen Douglas of Illinois was too much of an improviser; Charles Sumner of Massachusetts was devoured by moral fanaticism; Salmon P. Chase of Ohio was consumed by political ambitions; Alexander Stephens of Georgia, the strongest of Southern moderates, was too quick-tempered and inflexible. A plebiscite among the people in the North, South or West would have produced an overwhelming majority against any policy which might solve the slavery issue by war. No such plebiscite could have been held, for few men thought in terms of war. Instead, crisis succeeded crisis—the Kansas-Nebraska Act, 'Bleeding Kansas', the Dred Scott decision—while politicians sought to maintain the apparent interests of their sections. Tempers became inflamed and moderation diminished. Political leaders in North and South no longer had room to manœuvre and the nation blundered into war. It is only hindsight that allows us to see that the war was to settle two fundamental problems—slavery and the nature of the Union.

On these two matters the constitution was definite about slavery and ambiguous over states' rights. It explicitly guaranteed slavery in the clause about representation and in Article IV Section 2, which required fugitive slaves to be given up. It was the protection given to slavery which made an abolitionist condemn the constitution as a 'covenant with death, and an agreement with hell'. Yet there it was and Americans have always had an almost mystical devotion to their constitution, believing that the Founding Fathers knew best and that if it were only followed correctly it was bound to bring about the perfect society. This veneration of the constitution is particularly important in considering the cause of sectional conflict before the Civil War. Once the 'peculiar institution' of the South was regarded as conditioning all Southern attitudes and policies, and as anti-slavery feeling quickened in the North, it was inevitable that almost every question discussed in Congress would be liable to involve slavery. To the South slavery protected by the constitution had become the symbol of all their rights as a minority within the Union. If slavery was to be done away with, then what protection did a constitution once broken give for other rights? Northerners equally venerated the constitution and were not prepared to see it broken. Logically this meant that all that could be done about slavery was to hope that state action would get rid of it, as had been done by many Northern states by the beginning of the 19th century. But state action would obviously not occur in Southern states, and to rely on a change of heart there was patently intolerable for the abolitionists, to whom slavery was a heinous sin.

Thus unable to attack slavery directly they attacked it on the flank. The abolitionist influence in the political field was directed at gaining sympathizers in Congress who would raise peripheral matters about slavery on all occasions with wearisome iteration. Outright abolitionists were few throughout the country, and in Congress there were only a handful elected in the 1850's. These men were such as Gerrit Smith, Charles Sumner and Ben Wade, all of whom were fanatics unlikely to have been elected in normal times. But if abolitionists were few, there was a growing number of people in Congress and outside it who disliked slavery on moral grounds and wished to see it set on the path to ultimate extinction. These people were ready to support national campaigns. Those in Congress, while not joining in the vituperative abuse of the fanatics, were prepared to support measures against the extension of slavery. On certain matters the constitution said nothing or said something ambiguously; the status of slavery in the District of Columbia, the enforcement of the clause for the recovery of fugitive slaves, the internal slave trade and above all the extension of slavery into the new lands of the West. By raising these subjects they could harry slavery and hope to confine it to the area in which it already existed.

The political system of America encouraged this type of attack. There was, and in a sense still is, a fatal weakness in the working of this system. Initiative is, by the constitution, divided; the President may suggest but Congress must make the necessary laws. Only a strong and skilful President can impose his will on Congress and in the 19th century there was a tradition that the executive branch of government should exert itself as little as possible. This tradition was reinforced by a succession of weak Presidents. Pierce and Buchanan were chosen because they would not offend sectional interests by taking a strong line, thereby wrecking the unity of the national party. Harrison was selected as a conventional figurehead, while Tyler and Fillmore inherited the office through the death of their predecessors. Even Polk was nominated as a 'dark horse' and surprised everyone. Any politician who had spoken out strongly on the slavery issue was always ruled out as a Presidential candidate; even Abraham Lincoln in 1860 was chosen as the Republican candidate partly because his main rival Seward had been too outspoken in the past. Innocuous Presidents who had never offended any interest were the rule. Such Presidents usually fell into the hands of strong advisers who made use of the President's power in the interests of their own section. Thus did Jefferson Davis use his position as Secretary of War in Pierce's administration while Buchanan was the prey of the Southerners in his cabinet.

Even if there had been a President elected of tremendous character and political skill, capable of holding the loyalty of politicians from all sections, it would have been almost impossible for him to carry through a national plan to deal with slavery. Slavery heightened the sectional tension too rapidly and any general plan would have run into opposition. Radical opinion in the North would have resisted paying compensation to slave-owners; radical opinion in the South would not have considered anything. The vast majority of Americans were willing to drift along without any decision.

If the Presidency did not provide leadership Congress did not encourage constructive thought. As we have seen, Congressmen were really ambassadors for their sections. After 1840 political alignments steadily became more sectional and sectional divisions were duplicated in the Congressional committees—those small but powerful bodies which examined legislation in detail. Voting in these committees increasingly saw men separating as Northerners and Southerners, not as Whigs and Democrats, though party leaders tried hard to prevent this. Whigs were held together by the efforts of Henry Clay and Daniel Webster and only disintegrated in 1852. The Democratic party remained together until 1858, when Stephen Douglas and Buchanan split. Douglas, like Clay and Webster, worked continually for compromise. Every issue—price of land, routes of railways and the tariff—eventually was coloured by the slavery issue and Congressmen voted on them accordingly. Southerners were more solidly united, and resisted any measure of whatever kind proposed by Northerners. Constructive proposals to deal with slavery did not appear until it was too late and by then the tradition of compromise was breaking down. The tragic development of this situation is best seen by looking at the story of westward expansion. For the question of slavery in the territories was the most practical way in which the opponents and supporters of the institution could get results. Of all the methods of flank attacks on slavery in Congress it was the most important.

The story begins with the original thirteen colonies. Most of these possessed claims on Western lands on their borders. Between 1784 and 1786 Virginia, Massachusetts and Connecti-

ut, after considerable debate, surrendered their largest claims
o the Congress of the Articles of Confederation. One of the
ast acts of this Congress was to pass the North West Ordi-
ance in 1787, establishing a government for the area north
f the Ohio River. It was to be governed initially as a territory
vith a Governor and three judges appointed by Congress.
When there were 5,000 free adult males it could have a terri-
orial legislature and when 60,000 inhabitants existed it could
pply to Congress for admission as a state, on equal footing
vith the original thirteen. It was also laid down that from
hree to five states could be created in this North-West area,
nd that the existence of slavery was prohibited. This ordi-
ance was confirmed by the new Congress elected under the
ew Federal Constitution, and its main provisions have been
ollowed as the pattern for the expansion of America.[1]

The new constitution specifically stated that 'The Congress
hall have power to dispose of and make all needful rules and
egulations respecting the Territory or other property belong-
ng to the United States'. By this authority the South West
Ordinance was passed in 1790, organizing the lands south of
he Ohio. In this ordinance slavery was to be permitted. It
eemed, therefore, that the Ohio River had been made the
lividing line between slave and free states. Both Northerners
nd Southerners accepted this and no one questioned the right
f Congress to make rules about the existence of slavery in
ew territories. Slavery at this time appeared to be a dying
nstitution and this distinction between the North West Ordi-
ance and the South West Ordinance was simply a matter of
onvenience. Slaves were unlikely to be wanted north of the
Ohio, whereas they might be useful south of it. There followed
he Louisiana Purchase, and in due course new states applied
or admission. There was no problem over the provision per-
nitting or disallowing slavery as it was obvious in every case

[1] The Land Ordinance passed by Congress in 1785 under the
rticles of Confederation laid down the method by which Western
and was to be surveyed. It provided for townships six miles square,
ivided into 36 sections of 640 acres each. One section was to be
et aside for maintaining the local school. Thus the Articles of
Confederation were responsible for two fundamental ordinances.

whether the state was a slave or free area. Congress made similar provisions to those of the North West and South West Ordinances for the land in the Louisiana Purchase. In all, by 1819, Kentucky, Tennessee, Mississippi, Alabama and Louisiana were admitted as slave states and Vermont, Ohio, Indiana and Illinois as free states.

This made the number of slave and free states in the Union the same. But the free states had a larger population and had 105 members of the House of Representatives to the 81 of the slave states. In 1819 the territory of Missouri, which had been organized with no mention of slavery, applied for admission to the Union. It was a newly settled area lying further north than other slave territories and a motion was passed in the House of Representatives requiring that slavery should be abolished in Missouri before she was admitted. The existing slave states who had an equal vote in the Senate instantly made an outcry. Never before had Congress made such a condition for the admission of a state. Already the South was regarding the growing population of the North with alarm, and they were not prepared to accept being placed in a permanent minority in the Senate, by Missouri becoming free. A deadlock ensued for several months, which was finally broken by Maine applying for admission as a free state. Missouri was admitted without conditions and Congress imposed a general rule for the whole of the Louisiana territory by which, except for Missouri, slavery should be excluded north of a line 36° 30'. This meant that three-quarters of the Louisiana Purchase was destined to be free, but the slave states accepted this. Sectional lines were still fluid and the South did not foresee the great changes which would take place within the next twenty years. To Jefferson, however, the Missouri crisis was 'a firebell in the night', giving warning of disaster unless everyone took action.

The territorial question arose next when the drive westwards against Mexico brought further accessions of territory to the United States. By then, South Carolina had made her nullification stand over the tariff and the South acutely felt her minority status. The abolitionists had begun their propaganda which was to make slavery the major issue it had never been before. In the early 1820's American settlers had been moving

to Texas encouraged by the Mexican Government, who wel-
med industrious workers. By 1830 their numbers amounted
20,000 and the Mexican Government became alarmed at
is powerful group of foreigners. They prohibited further im-
igration and imposed various laws restraining the activities
the existing Americans.[2] New settlers continued to arrive
d a state of friction resulted reaching a climax in open war
tween 1835 and 1836. The heroic siege of the Alamo, a mis-
n station in San Antonio where 188 Texans, including Davy
rockett, resisted 4,000 Mexicans for a fortnight, was followed
a total defeat of the Mexican Army. Sam Houston, the
exan general, forced Mexico to accept the independence of
exas, thus creating the Lone Star Republic. But the Texans
d not wish to remain independent and in 1837 petitioned
e United States for annexation. President Jackson was not
epared to have a war with Mexico on his hands and the
fer was refused.

Several years passed and in 1844 President Tyler, fearing
e growing connection between Texas and Great Britain,
ade a treaty of annexation with Texas but it was defeated in
e Senate by 35 votes to 16. The size of the vote was primarily
ie to Northern opposition to a great increase in the area of
e slave states. In the election of 1844 the Democrats skil-
lly linked the Texas question with that of Oregon where
ousands of Americans had settled in the past fifty years. The
udson's Bay Company exercised authority in the area and
ie new American settlers were determined to have a govern-
ent of their own. Britain was prepared to accept a boundary
ie along the Columbia River, but the Democratic Presidential
indidate, James K. Polk, raised the cry '54° 40' or fight'. He
ished in on the rising tide of American expansion usually
iown as 'Manifest Destiny'—the destiny of Americans to oc-
ipy the whole North American continent. Polk won the elec-
on; Texas was admitted as a state with the Missouri com-
romise provision as to slavery even before Polk took office.
/ithin a year of his doing so the United States was at war
ith Mexico, mainly on account of the Mexican Government's
fusal to negotiate on the Texan boundaries and to consider

[2] Compare the Uitlanders in the Transvaal, before the Boer War.

an American offer to buy California into which great number
of settlers had already moved. The war could probably have
been prevented with patience and it was denounced by mos
Whig politicians including Lincoln,[3] as unnecessary and un
provoked. By September 1847, United States' troops had oc
cupied Mexico City and in the next year a treaty of peace was
made by which the United States acquired California and the
area then known as New Mexico. Fifteen million dollars were
paid by the United States and Mexico surrendered all claim
to Texas.

In 1846, while the war was in progress, Polk had introduced
a bill to raise two million dollars with which to negotiate with
Mexico. In the House of Representatives a Democratic Con
gressman from Pennsylvania, David Wilmot, had proposed a
proviso to be added to this bill, stating quite clearly that slav
ery would not be permitted in any territory acquired from
Mexico. This Wilmot Proviso was killed by the Senate after
the House had supported it by 87 votes to 64. An attempt by
others to get the Missouri compromise line extended was de
feated. For three years off and on the crisis raged in Congress
and the Press. In the Presidential election of 1848 leaders of
both parties attempted to sidetrack the slavery issue; the Dem
ocrats chose a candidate from Michigan, the Whigs a planter
from Louisiana. But once the election was over the need to
establish a government for California, where the gold rush of
1848 had enormously multiplied the population, brought the
whole question once more to the front. Northern and Southern
Churches split in two, all but one Northern legislature supported the Wilmot Proviso and from the South came stern
warnings of secession. Calhoun, the veteran leader from South
Carolina, foretold that with the South becoming a minority in
the Union, her constitutional rights must be respected. 'All we
ask is to be let alone; but if trampled upon it will be idle to
expect that we will not resist it.' The North accused the South
of aggression in extending the slave power; the South listed
acts of aggression by the North in impeding the return of

[3] Then serving for his first and only term in the House of Representatives.

ugitive slaves, and in proposing to exclude slaves from the erritories.

In the end the efforts of the two great compromisers, Daniel Webster and Henry Clay, produced a solution. All matters were brought together into one great compromise, passed, however, in separate bills on the suggestion of Stephen Douglas from Illinois. It was this suggestion which enabled sufficient support to be secured for each individual measure. By these measures, California was admitted as a free state, and Utah and New Mexico were organized as territories with no provision about slavery except the pledge 'that when admitted as a state, the said territory or any portion of the same, shall be received into the Union, with or without slavery as their constitution may prescribe at the time of their admission'. A Fugitive Slave Law established Federal commissioners who could enforce the recapture of fugitives with the aid of heavy penalties; the slave trade was prohibited in the District of Columbia although slavery continued to be permitted there. Thus the matter appeared settled: all the peripheral matters seemed decided by law and no room was left for ambiguity. The great majority viewed the compromise of 1850 as a permanent settlement and breathed a sigh of relief. Northern radicals indeed gave warning that they were not content and would obstruct the Fugitive Slave Law and would appeal to a 'higher law' than that contained in the constitution. But in the South, the extremists were sharply defeated in the state elections of 1851.

Yet the calm which succeeded the storms of the two preceding years was deceptive. The Southern editorial, 'Let no southern man be deceived; a momentary quiet has hushed the voice of agitation but there is no peace', was prophetic. But the election of 1852 saw general approval for the compromise. There were now general rules about slavery covering all the United States: (i) self-determination in existing states; (ii) the line 36° 30′ in the Louisiana Purchase and (iii) nonintervention by Congress in the lands acquired from Mexico. Would this not end the whole question? Unfortunately, dangerous differences still remained. There were in fact three different views about slavery in the territories. In the opinion of the extreme Southerner, since the constitution protected prop-

erty, a citizen of any state could take his slaves into any terri
tory. A territorial government had no right to prohibit slaver
until it applied for admission as a state; if necessary, Congres
must intervene to protect slavery before that. Thus congres
sional non-intervention was strictly limited; Congress must nc
intervene to prohibit slavery, but if a territory sought to do sc
Congress must then intervene to prevent such a prohibition
The second view was that of Douglas: that the people of
territory should decide and that Congress had no right of in
tervention. As we shall see, Douglas believed that this princip]
of popular sovereignty had superseded the line 36° 30'. F:
nally there was the Northern belief that the territories of th
United States belonged to the people of the Union as a whole
and that Congress had a positive right and a duty to exclud
slavery from these territories.

The Northern view could not be reconciled with the othe
two, but the compromise of 1850 had successfully defeated i
The difficulty lay in the contradiction between the Southerner
and Douglas. Both had accepted the compromise but in di:
ferent senses. Looking back, it appears a singularly barren cor
troversy, but what was at stake to the South was their whol
position as a minority. As William L. Yancey was to say i
1860 at the Charleston Convention, 'We claim the benefit c
the Constitution that was made for the protection of minoritie
In the march of events, feeling conscious of your numerica
power, you have aggressed upon us. We hold up between u
and your advancing columns of numbers that written instru
ment which your fathers made and the compact by which yo
with your powers were to respect us and our rights.' An
from the constitution the South had a strong legal and logica
viewpoint. The Northerners could only proceed with their po]
cies by violating the strict logic of the constitution, and ap
pealing as Seward did to a higher law.

All this made the finality of the 1850 compromise wishfu
thinking since the South, as a minority, felt forced to prote
its rights and claim the full measure of them under the const:
tution, although it was obvious that those rights would n
add one slave state to the Union. But that was not the real
important point in the last resort. Though the ordinary ma

settled down thankfully after 1850, signs were not wanting of trouble to come. The Fugitive Slave Law was blatantly disobeyed in the North, and in June 1851 the first instalment of *Uncle Tom's Cabin* appeared. This sentimental novel, written by a New England mother, did more than anything else to spread the stereotyped picture of the brutality of the slave system. The Presidential election of 1852 saw the last appearance of the two national parties; Democratic leadership lay increasingly in the hands of Southerners, and the party was strengthened by recruits from the Whigs of the South who felt with Robert Toombs of Georgia that 'we can never have peace and security with Seward, Greeley & Co. in the ascendant of our party counsels'. This breakdown of the Whig party left the way open for a new party, based purely on sectional lines. Once sectional parties arose, the forces of compromise which had triumphed in 1850 would find it increasingly difficult to maintain a compromise.

It is only hindsight which emphasizes these portents of future trouble. Most contemporaries were surprised when the next crisis came. In the event it came unexpectedly and its author was Stephen Douglas. This senator from Illinois was one of the most striking politicians of the day. Known as the 'little Giant' from his enormous head on a small body, he was a forceful and intelligent personality. Born in Vermont, he had gone westwards to Illinois where he had practised law and entered politics. In 1847 he had become a senator and in the compromise of 1850 he had been closely linked with Clay. Still under forty, he appeared to have a dazzling career before him. He had married a wealthy and beautiful wife; business interests had made him rich; and he was by far the most influential of all Northern Democrats. Illinois had considerable Southern sympathies and Douglas received strong support for all policies favouring compromise between the sections. If he could maintain his influence over Southern Democrats as well, his chances of reaching the Presidency were bright. So not only did national but also personal interest recommend compromise to him.

Opinions about Douglas have often been harsh. In his own day, he was attacked by men in both North and South for having no moral sense, for personal ambition and for corrupt business deals. Admittedly his conduct was frequently lax and he was above all an improviser. He was no theorist and treated all matters as ones to be settled by trial and error. Believing passionately in Manifest Destiny and democracy, he felt that the native good sense of the American people would settle the issue of slavery without bringing morality into it. As America expanded, slavery would die out in territories to which it was not suited. He was the one major political figure in the last decade before the Civil War who tried to treat the issue of slavery as a practical reality. He believed, and probably rightly, that the limits of slavery were already drawn by nature. What need, therefore, to make Congress declare a principle of the moral right or wrong of slavery? Let Congress say nothing, and allow the people of each territory to make their own decision. Neither North nor South had anything to gain in practice by enforcing a principle and the Union had everything to lose by such action.

In the Senate, Douglas was Chairman of the Joint Committee on Territories. For many years there had been pressure to organize the territory west of Iowa and Missouri. Dissatisfied settlers in these two states were eager to move west and wished the new land to be properly organized. Railway financiers, anxious to promote a central route for a transcontinental railroad, supported a new territorial organization able to attract settlers. The outcome of these and other pressures was that early in the first session of the 33rd Congress in the spring of 1854, J. G. Miller, a Congressman from Missouri, and Senator Dodge of Iowa introduced a bill to organize the territory of Nebraska. This bill was naturally referred to Douglas's Committee, which recommended that the basic principles of the compromise of 1850 should be put into practical effect by organizing it as two territories, Kansas and Nebraska, as it was too large for only one. All questions pertaining to slavery in these two territories were to be left to the decision of the people residing in them. All questions involving ownership of slaves were to be referred to local tribunals, and the Fugitive Slave Law was to have effect.

All would have been well but for the fact that the two ter

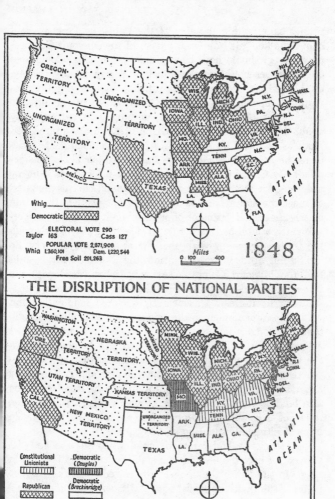

1848

Whig ▭
Democratic ▨

ELECTORAL VOTE 290
Taylor 163   Cass 127
POPULAR VOTE 2,871,908
Whig 1,360,101   Dem. 1,220,544
Free Soil 291,263

Miles
0   100   400

THE DISRUPTION OF NATIONAL PARTIES

1860

Constitutional Unionists ▥
Republican ▨
Democratic (Douglas) ▤
Democratic (Breckinridge) ▤

ELECTORAL VOTE 303
Lincoln 180, Bell 39, Douglas 12, Breckinridge 72
POPULAR VOTE 4,676,853
Rep. 1,866,352, Dem. (Douglas) 1,375,157, Dem. (Breckinridge) 847,514
C.U. 587,380

Miles
100   400

ritories came within the area of the Louisiana Purchase and
above the line 36° 30′. On the basis of the Missouri Compromise slavery should have been prohibited. But the Committee
on Territories held that the principle of popular sovereignty,
established in 1850, was a new principle *superseding* the geographical line of the Missouri Compromise. In the original
draft of the bill as it appeared, nothing was said explicitly
about this, but when Senator Dixon of Kentucky approached
Douglas and said he intended to offer an amendment to declare the Missouri Compromise unconstitutional, Douglas replied: 'By God, sir, you are right; I will incorporate it in my
bill, tho' I know it will raise a hell of a storm'. He was prepared
to meet the storm because he believed it was worth stating
clearly that the doctrine of popular sovereignty had been permanently established as a rule to deal with slavery through
the United States—in established states and new territory. So
the fateful words were written into the Kansas-Nebraska Bill;
that the Missouri Compromise 'being inconsistent with the
principle of non-intervention by Congress with slavery in the
states or territories . . . is hereby declared inoperative and
void'. This amendment to the original bill was suggested neither by Douglas nor by the Southern leaders. But Douglas
approved of it when it was suggested. He believed so passionately in the idea of popular sovereignty that he was prepared, whatever the storm, to have it proclaimed. Despising
the holding of abstract principles in others, he had now fallen
into holding them himself. For he was willing to accept the
repeal of an established compromise (the Missouri) in the vain
hope of ultimately silencing all objections.

The storm he had foreseen broke with violence and destroyed for ever the illusion that stability had been reached in
1850. In the North the abolitionists seized upon the Kansas-
Nebraska Bill with its repeal of the Missouri Compromise as a
fresh example of a slave plot. Chase and Sumner, their leaders,
having asked Douglas to delay discussion in the Senate, had
spent the interval in producing a vehement protest, 'The Appeal of the Independent Democrats', in which they spoke of
a monstrous plot and a gross violation of a sacred pledge. It
was printed and circulated to every clergyman in the North

and rapidly became accepted as the truth. The Kansas-Nebraska Act became the climax of Southern aggression, the latest proof of a gigantic slave conspiracy. The New England Emigrant Aid Society was formed to promote the settlement of anti-slavery groups in the new territories. In July, meetings were held in Jackson, Michigan, out of which came the formation of a new party, called Republican, dedicated to preventing the extension of slavery. Thus did the Kansas Act solidify opinion in the North and bring about the formation of a sectional party. In effect, the bill was to the North what John Brown's raid was to be to the South; both confirmed fears and suspicions already felt.

But if the South had a certain justice in its fears in that John Brown had the practical support of prominent abolitionists, the North had no right to claim that the Kansas-Nebraska Bill was part of a Southern plot. As Sam Houston of Texas said, 'The South has not asked for it . . .'; the New Orleans 'Crescent' called the bill 'this indiscreet injudicious and uncalled for measure'. Once passed, however, obviously all Southerners were prepared to accept it as it supported their constitutional claims. Yet the evidence increasingly shows that the South as a whole were indifferent until the fury of the North in attributing motives to the South made them begin to act upon these motives. But even so, while the New England states poured men and money into Kansas, the response from the South in doing the same was feeble. Kansas, before these new settlers arrived, was in a natural condition of frontier turbulence; the land survey was not yet finished, bandits and Indians pillaged continuously. It was a scene which could easily be twisted to fit the pattern of the pro-slavery and the abolition parties. 'Bleeding Kansas' existed even before it became an arena for sectional antagonisms. John Brown, a lawless ne'er-do-well, massacred pro-slavery settlers at Pottawatomie, not so much to strike a blow at slavery as to prevent the establishment of orderly government in an area which was a paradise to the lawless. Even President Buchanan's misguided acceptance of the Lecompton constitution,[4] drawn up by a minority of Kansas settlers, can be defended on the ground

[4] See p. 77.

that some territorial government had to be recognized in order to prevent further disorder.

Complicated though the story of the Kansas-Nebraska Act is, it is the turning-point in the sectional conflict. The bases on which the compromise of 1850 had been accepted were broken. They might have been destroyed without Kansas but there is a great deal to be said in times of passion for trying to delay crises. The danger after 1854 for the American Union was that crises came speedily one after another, and no time was allowed for passions to subside. The Kansas-Nebraska Act convinced the North of the existence of a Southern plot; it was after its passage that Garrison wrote: 'What is the South but one vast graveyard? Monsters whose arguments are the bowie knife and the revolver, tar and feathers, the lash, the bludgeon, the halter and the stake.' Moreover, it was owing to the Act that the Republican party was formed. The South for their part became convinced that the North intended to deny them their rights, and under pressure of Northern attacks, Southerners were increasingly willing to listen to the voice of the Southern extremists, demanding the last inch of their constitutional rights. Common sense no longer had much to do with it as each section imputed aggressive designs to the other; every proposal became a plot and every act a threat.

The course of sectional conflict after 1854 is soon told. The 34th Congress, which met in December 1854, remained for two and a half months without a Speaker and was thus unable to conduct any business, so high did tempers rise. Throughout 1855, the story of 'Bleeding Kansas' continued to inflame sectional strife. In the spring of 1856, Charles Sumner made an abstract and bombastic speech on the 'Crime against Kansas'. This prompted a young Congressman from South Carolina, Preston Brooks, to enter the Senate Chamber and attack Sumner with a cane, belabouring him over the head. Sumner retired hurt, and did not appear again in the Senate until December 1859. Violence in Kansas was thus paralleled by violence in Congress itself. In the Presidential election of 1856, John C. Frémont, the first candidate of the Republican party, a soldier and explorer of fame, stood on a platform maintaining the power of Congress to exclude slavery from the territories.

He gained 1,335,264 votes against the 1,838,169 of his Democratic rival, James Buchanan, whose platform affirmed the compromise of 1850 and the Kansas-Nebraska Act as 'the only sound and safe solution of the slavery question'. Two days after Buchanan's inauguration in March 1857 came the Supreme Court's decision on the Dred Scott case.

Scott had been born a slave in Virginia in 1795. He had moved with his master to Missouri and had been sold to an army surgeon who had taken him as a household servant to his posts at Rock Island in Illinois and Fort Snelling in the territory of Wisconsin. In Illinois slavery was prohibited by the North West Ordinance of 1787, and in Wisconsin by the Missouri Compromise. Claiming to be a citizen of Missouri, Scott based his case on having lived on free soil from 1834 to 1838 in Illinois and Wisconsin. He first made application to the courts in 1846 and for over eight years his case remained in lower courts before reaching the Supreme Court of the United States in 1854. Not until 1856 did it reach a final hearing. Scott had been sick and inefficient for many years, and his legal owner, an army surgeon's widow who lived in New York, finding him an embarrassment, put no obstacle in the way of the anti-slavery interests anxious to push Scott's case. The case involved three main issues: whether Scott was a citizen of Missouri and therefore able to sue in a Federal court; whether his temporary stay on free soil entitled him to remain permanently free, even when he returned to a slave state; and, finally, the general validity of the Missouri Compromise. Moreover, it arose at a time when there was hot debate in the country whether either Congress or a territorial legislature had the right to prohibit slavery.

The Supreme Court could have dealt with the matter simply by deciding that Scott as a slave was not a citizen and therefore could not sue. There was no need for them to pronounce on the more controversial issues. However, under the guidance of the aged Chief Justice Taney of Maryland, the majority opinion of the Court went on to pronounce on the whole question of slavery in the territories. In a verbose and confused judgement, it supported the extreme Southern constitutional position that any law excluding slavery from the territories was unconstitutional. Taney, who had quite unethically had conversations on the subject with Buchanan, hoped thus to settle a great national question as had been done in the past by Supreme Court decisions. The Supreme Court after all was the guardian of the sacred constitution, and its decision must be accepted by every section of the country. Unfortunately, this hope entirely ignored the political realities; the North, the East and the Middle West would not accept a judgement which so flagrantly violated their most deeply held beliefs. Not only to Republicans, but also to Douglas Democrats, the Dred Scott decision was anathema. The former simply refused to accept it and appealed to a higher law above the constitution. The latter were driven to expound the so-called Freeport doctrine (named from the place where Douglas delivered a speech) by which it was held that though the Supreme Court might be constitutionally correct, in practice slavery could only exist where the territorial legislatures passed slave codes to protect it. If they refused to do so, the Dred Scott decision would remain a dead letter. By such an argument, Douglas strove to maintain his ideal of popular sovereignty. In face of this Freeport doctrine, Southerners began to demand in Congress the passage of a Federal slave code to protect slavery in the territories. In making this demand they reached the full logical extent of Southern claims.

The Dred Scott decision was fateful because it encouraged Southerners to rely on their legal rights under the constitution, and made compromise impossible. Before the decision, compromise over the status of slavery was still possible, since the constitution had appeared to speak with an uncertain voice on the matter. Under Buchanan's régime, the South appeared to have everything its own way. He was an irresolute President, allowing himself to be ruled by a mediocre Cabinet in which Southern opinion was dominant. This Southern opinion was encouraged in its extreme claims by the financial panic of the summer of 1857. The North with its commerce and industry suffered badly, whereas the South, secure in its European cotton trade, weathered the storm surprisingly well. It appeared as if the American Union depended for its economic stability on the South and its peculiar institution. In December 1858,

Buchanan accepted the Lecompton constitution for Kansas. This had been designed by a minority of Kansas settlers and permitted slavery. The bulk of free soil settlers had boycotted the Lecompton meeting, and Buchanan, by accepting the constitution, was flagrantly violating the principle of popular sovereignty. But apart from the urgent need to provide some government for the territory, it appeared to offer an opportunity to assert Southern claims to equality in the territories. Douglas was as incensed as the Republicans at Buchanan's action. He demanded that the President, whom he despised, should withdraw his support and was answered with the words, 'Mr. Douglas, I desire you to remember that no Democrat ever yet differed from an administration without being crushed'. Douglas's revolt did not result in his being crushed, but it irretrievably split the Democratic party. The administration withdrew its support from all Douglas Democrats, and Douglas campaigned in Congress and throughout the country against the Lecompton constitution. A compromise was at last reached by which the constitution was to be submitted to all the inhabitants of Kansas. In August 1858 the vote was held and it was overwhelmingly for rejection.[5] Once more the practical futility of the Southern claims was seen; the Dred Scott decision had made no practical difference to the spread of slavery and the Lecompton constitution merely served to exasperate the North and split the Democratic party, without making Kansas a slave state.

The breach between Douglas and Buchanan marks the moment when the Democratic party became a sectional one. Douglas was left as the leader of Northern and Western Democrats who were to vote for him in 1860 and not for Lincoln. Buchanan and his advisers in breaking with Douglas had once again judged wrongly. They had felt that they could discipline Douglas and thereby keep control of North-Western Democracy. Only thus could Southern interests retain control of the Presidency. But this was a gross misreading of the political forces and a woeful failure of statesmanship. The one chance of the South was to keep the Democratic party united. The Republicans, a sectional party, could never hope to win in

[5] 11,812 against 1,926.

1860 unless there was a divided Democracy. Concessions rather than threats to Douglas were needed, but Southern leaders, blinded by the strength of their constitutional position, were not prepared to make concessions.

With the growth of sectional parties, the story of sectional conflict is virtually told. There were now two sectional parties, each taking the initiative and leaving no place in them for the millions of moderates who to the very last moment sought, by voting in 1860 for Douglas or for Bell's Constitutional Union party, to avert disaster. The disruption of parties meant the breakdown of the whole democratic process, yet the process still continued. In the late summer and autumn of 1858 occurred the mid-term elections. The most famous contest was between Lincoln and Douglas in Illinois for the Senate. Seven debates were held between the two men during the campaign and in the course of them every aspect of the slavery controversy was covered. In one of them, at Freeport, Douglas enunciated his doctrine. Lincoln lost the contest by a narrow margin but emerged as a national figure condemning slavery as 'a moral, a social and a political wrong', which must be put on the path of ultimate extinction by limiting its expansion through congressional action. He raised the debate to a higher level by claiming that the United States still represented a new hope for mankind. A house divided against itself could not stand and all Americans were concerned with the issue of slavery whose existence undermined the foundations of their democratic Union. It was not simply a matter for the South, or for the settlers of any particular territory to decide.

Elsewhere the elections resulted in the Republicans gaining 18 seats in the House of Representatives. With the Douglas Democrats the Republicans now controlled the House. The administration still had a majority in the Senate[6] but the signs were ominous for the South in the Presidential election year of 1860. The eyes of political leaders everywhere became fixed on this event. In October 1859 came the crazy attack by John Brown on the Federal arsenal at Harper's Ferry. Having obtained money from certain Northern abolitionists Brown

[6] In February 1860, Jefferson Davis succeeded in getting through the Senate resolutions embodying the full Southern view on slavery.

planned to start a slave insurrection in Virginia and establish a free state as a bridgehead to continue the rebellion southwards. In the event he captured the arsenal at Harper's Ferry with eighteen men including five Negroes. No slaves came to his support and after a two-day siege Brown surrendered to a Federal force under the command of Colonel Robert E. Lee. He was tried for treason against the state of Virginia and was hanged on December 2nd. Anti-slavery groups throughout the North mourned him as a martyr, although the majority of Northerners condemned the raid. In the South there was deep alarm, and their leaders could point to the raid as justifying the worst fears of what would happen under a Republican administration. In both North and South John Brown's raid could hardly be ignored as a sign that the times were out of joint and that the tradition of compromise was giving way to force. Yet the signs were ignored; to most Americans secession and Civil War were wholly unexpected when they came, despite two decades of fierce sectional conflict. The nation as a whole was deaf to the warnings uttered by the extremists on both sides and blind to the omens of disaster. Optimism and credulity combined to disguise the fact that the choice of the next President of the United States would be a fateful decision.

CHAPTER V

THE CAUSES OF SECESSION

By 1860 sectional political parties had replaced national ones, yet it was still possible to believe that some reconciliation of differing interests could be achieved. The situation was indeed dangerous but not fatal to the existence of the American Union. It might become fatal if Southerners made good their long-reiterated threat of secession. But the very fact that this threat, so often repeated, had never yet been implemented gave Northerners and moderates the illusion that it never would be. This illusion was dangerous and the North might not have persisted in holding it, if the mind and temper of the South, developed in the past generation, had been better understood.

For the past thirty years the South had been well educated by its publicists and politicians in the full doctrine of states' rights which was their constitutional defence as a minority against the aggression of a majority. This doctrine was not in theory incompatible with loyalty to the Union. Nothing could be further from the truth. States' rights simply involved an interpretation of the constitution which could be justified in logic and by history. Supporters of the theory, whether in Virginia in 1798, New England in 1814 or South Carolina in 1830, considered the Federal government to be an agent of the sovereign states, entrusted with certain carefully defined powers for the performance of specific duties. The states had never surrendered their sovereignty or agreed to unlimited submission to the government created by the original compact. If the Federal government at any time usurped authority beyond the limits of its delegated powers, each state then had the right to determine for itself the nature and extent of remedial measures. It was the nature of all delegated power to increase and a majority could thus continuously oppress the minority, un-

less that minority had a self-protecting power. In 1814 the
New England states suggested constitutional reform as the
remedy; in 1830 South Carolina invoked the doctrine of Nullification. The ultimate remedy was secession and by the logic
of this narrow interpretation of the constitution it was a per-
fectly legitimate step.

From 1830 onwards the South had felt itself to be a minority
faced by a steadily advancing industrial North. That the South
had control of Congress and the Supreme Court did not alter
this feeling, and the best political talent in the South was ex-
erted to preserve the Union by seeking acknowledgement of
the constitutional safeguards allowed to them. John C. Calhoun of South Carolina and the three great Georgian politicians—Alexander Stephens, Robert Toombs and Howell Cobb
—were all of them prominent Unionists. Stephens, indeed, is
the best example of the Southern dilemma. On November
14th, 1860, when the tide of secession was already rising, this
pale-faced attenuated little man made an impassioned plea in
the Georgia legislature advising his state not to secede. Yet
when it did he followed it and became the unhappy, thwarted
Vice-President of the Confederacy, seldom appearing in Richmond and usually remaining at his home in Georgia—'My native land, my country; the only one that is country to me is
Georgia'. After the war he spent his last years writing the vast
and exhaustive *Constitutional View of the Late War between
the States* which was really a treatise on the origins of the
Federal Constitution. In the frail person of Stephens the tension of Unionism and states' rights is tragically revealed, a tension which the North never fully comprehended and which
Lincoln and Seward underestimated when they placed reliance
on the well-known strength of Union sentiment in the South
during the vital months between November 1860 and April
1861.[1] In the crisis 'my country' meant 'my state' to the vast
majority of Southerners.

In considering the cause of secession during the winter of
1860–61 it is necessary to distinguish clearly between states'
rights men and the fire-eaters or Southern nationalists as they
are better called. The former regarded secession as a consti-

[1] See below, p. 102.

tutional right which might in dire necessity be invoked: the latter regarded it as a positive good to be used as soon as possible in the creation of a Southern nation; to them safeguards for the Southern economic and social order were impossible to find within the framework of the existing Union. The Southern nationalists in the period up to 1856 were not the political leaders of the South. Few of them had made a notable mark in politics and many of them were fanatics out of step with the general current of Southern opinion. South Carolina was the nationalists' home, generally in plantations along the coast. Robert J. Turnbull agitated in the 1820's and 1830's. Robert Barnwell Rhett, a fiery orator with a poor plantation, inherited Turnbull's mantle and through his editorial control of the Charleston *Mercury* pressed continuously for a Southern confederacy. The Virginian, Edmund Ruffin, caught the infection when he was making an agricultural survey of South Carolina. The cause of Southern nationalism became his passion and it was he who, as a volunteer of sixty-five, fired the first gun against Fort Sumter, and who, after the defeat of Lee's army, wrapped himself in a Confederate flag and shot himself through the brain, having inscribed these last words in his diary: 'I here repeat and would willingly proclaim my unmitigated hatred to Yankee rule, and to all political, social and business connection with Yankees, and the perfidious, malignant and vile Yankee race'.

The idea of a separate Southern nation was obviously in the realm of a fevered imagination until the Mexican acquisitions opened up the possibility of a Southern state which might exist on almost equal terms with the North. The new territories were considerably larger than the total area with which the United States in 1783 had begun its existence. A new prospect was opened up, and certain politicians from the South-West became leading exponents of the idea. This was the opportunity for the parvenu South, rude in its culture and engaged in a mad scramble for wealth, to lead a movement of its own against the Northern states. That there was a Northern nation, intensely concentrated in sympathy and purpose, was evident: why not establish a Southern nation, just as widespread, just as unified and based on the fact of slavery?

It was actually the sons of South Carolina who directed this campaign. William Lowndes Yancey, leading exponent of secession, was a South Carolina planter who had become bankrupt. He had migrated to Alabama where he found a new career in law, politics and agitation. James de Bow had also migrated from South Carolina to Louisiana where he had started a commercial review to publicize the economic foundations for a new nation. Louis T. Wigfall, also born in South Carolina, had made his career in Texas, becoming for a while its United States senator. He possessed a bitter tongue, and a talent for self-advertisement which often found an outlet in physical violence against personal opponents.[2] From South Carolina itself the rotund and voluble senator, J. H. Hammond, publicist of the phrase 'King Cotton', maintained the cause. But the main leader was the future President of the Confederacy—the austere and humourless Jefferson Davis.[3] Born in Kentucky within a year and a hundred miles of Lincoln, he had been transplanted by the kindness of an elder brother to a rich plantation at Natchez on the Mississippi. He entered politics, becoming a senator and Secretary of War in Pierce's administration. Though of a different type to Yancey and Wigfall he saw a future for the South as an independent nation. Cabinet office moderated his enthusiasm for a time but by 1860 he, together with his fellow senators from neighbouring Louisiana, Judah P. Benjamin and John Slidell, represented the Southern extremists in Congress. All of them were men who had risen from humble beginnings, fighting for their ambition all along the line. The land of the South-West, where they lived, was rich with newly acquired wealth, and its inhabitants were self-assertive and arrogant behind a veneer of older Southern culture. It was from here that the elements which gave rise to the Confederacy existed. They may have talked the language of states' rights but their accent was not that of John C. Calhoun and their goal was not to prevent secession but to secure it.

It is this basic division within the South which explains both the rise and the fall of the Confederacy. The New South personified by Alabama was interested in separation. Yet the new

[2] See p. 108.
[3] See p. 134.

nation created at Montgomery, Alabama, in February 1861, was to be in part destroyed by the stubborn states' rights tradition, maintained throughout the war particularly by Georgia and North Carolina. Jefferson Davis treated his government as if it were a national one and found that the genuine states' rights men objected to this as much as they had done in the old Union. W. H. Russell, the English correspondent for *The Times*, had observed in 1861 that 'a strong government must be the logical consequence of victory and the triumph of the South will be attended by a similar result for which indeed many Southerners are well disposed'. But equally many Southerners were not well disposed; to them the war was a necessity forced on them by the need to defend their constitutional rights, as Alexander Stephens argued in his monumental book. But to the men of the South-West it was a war for Southern independence rather than for the defence of states' rights. Independence all along had been a conscious aim and purpose.

It is this division between the political leaders of the South, men speaking the same language but meaning different things by it, which explains why sectional conflict eventually brought secession. It is often forgotten how near the South came to secession in 1850. A time of crisis was the moment for the fire-eaters and in the crisis over the Mexican acquisitions and the Wilmot Proviso they had a superb opportunity. Northern attacks on slavery had unified the South and temporarily hidden its divisions. Unionists talked of secession but in their hearts thought of it as a weapon to persuade the North to grant constitutional rights; Southern nationalists talked of secession and meant it. If the North would not give way the game would be in the hands of the extremists, for the Unionists would either have to admit that their secession talk was bluff or accept the direction of those who would not give way.

The Unionists sought to control the movement by the policy of co-operative secession—that all states should meet in convention and decide on joint action. Southern nationalists pressed for immediate action by individual states, thereby hoping to push matters to an extreme when they had the example to brandish of one state leaving the Union. The Unionists prevailed and a call was issued for a general convention of the

Southern states to meet at Nashville, Tennessee, in June 1850. When it met, Clay's compromise measures were already before Congress, and the edge was taken from the extremists' axe. The Unionists were able to secure general acceptance for the compromise coupled with warnings to the North that Southern rights in future must be in no way denied. A general wave of relief passed through the South and in succeeding state elections the fire-eaters were largely discredited. Mississippi elected the Unionist Foote in preference to Jefferson Davis, while Yancey lost his fight in Alabama to the more moderate Hilliard. The Union party swept Georgia with a thoroughness that could not be mistaken and Virginians refused to listen to Ruffin. Even in South Carolina moderate men carried the day.

The movement for Southern independence seemed thus to be but a flash in the pan. Whether it returned with explosive force depended in large measure on the North. There was bitter disappointment in many disunionist hearts but Jefferson Davis reflected more wisely. He ceased to be an out-and-out secessionist and became instead an extreme advocate of Southern rights within the Union. He still thought in terms of Southern imperialism, and as Secretary of War in Franklin Pierce's Cabinet he was instrumental in securing the Gadsden Purchase[4] to assist a Southern railroad and was also a leading spirit in the openly proclaimed determination of the Pierce administration to annex Cuba. A great powerful South protected by all the safeguards of the constitution, resting on slavery as its economic foundation and strengthened if necessary by a revived slave trade—this was Davis's new ambition. It was an ambition which only secession could make possible and it was still essentially an ambition of the New South, not the Old South.

The extremists came to the fore again once sectional conflict revived in its full bitterness in 1854. They could claim 'to have told you so'. Their activities were aimed at educating Southerners for independence. They emphasized the South's funda-

---

[4] In 1853 James Gadsden negotiated a treaty with Mexico to buy a strip of territory for 15 million dollars. The treaty was ratified in 1854 at a price of 10 million dollars.

mental viability, praising King Cotton and pointing out the North's economic weakness particularly in 1857 when the South remained largely unaffected by the slump which engulfed both Europe and the Northern States. Plans were set on foot to establish direct trade with Europe, thus cutting out the Northern middleman. Campaigns were launched to keep Southern sons at home for college and to give them Southern text-books and Southern periodicals. Writers set to work to prove the superiority of Southern institutions. Schemers like the Knights of the Golden Circle planned to annex lands in the Caribbean and Mexico for the new nation.

In 1856, when the full danger of the Republican party was seen—a sectional party dedicated to the limitation of slavery extension—the nationalists strengthened their position. Had they not for over three decades warned the South that this would happen? The Republicans were a party of abolitionists who sought to destroy Southern society. Had they not circulated Helper's cruel book, *The Impending Crisis*, in an attempt to foment a slave war? Were they not refusing to return slaves to their rightful owners despite the provisions of the Fugitive Slave Law? It is easy to see the power of these arguments in the conditions of the time. In State assemblies, in rural townships, in local newspapers and in the recently founded annual commercial conventions, the nationalists were in the forefront of the argument. The initiative was on their side to promote drastic action; the Unionists could only call for patience and for confidence in the constitution and the Supreme Court which the Republican party had already declared they did not intend to obey.

There are then by 1859 three distinguishable groups in the politics of the South: the fire-eaters or nationalists; the Southern rights party who pressed for full Southern rights under the constitution; and the Southern Unionists. All talked of states' rights but meant different things by what they said. The hope of peace lay with the last group; the chance of war with the first. The middle group would follow the first if their rights were not granted (and it was inevitable that they would not be). The three groups could be symbolized by Yancey, Jeffer-

son Davis[5] and Alexander Stephens. Yet in the conventions
held to nominate the Presidential candidates for 1860 these
divisions were not important. The Democratic party met in
April in the fateful city of Charleston, South Carolina. The followers of Douglas who were mainly Northerners or former
Whigs carried the convention against the Southerners. The
delegations of eight Southern states then seceded from the convention and in June nominated their own candidate, John C.
Breckinridge of Kentucky, on a platform supporting the extreme Southern claims within the Union. Douglas had been
nominated on a platform demanding non-intervention by Congress on the matter of slavery. The remnants of the old Whig
party nominated John Bell of Tennessee on a platform which
avoided the slavery issue by simply stating that it upheld 'the
Constitution of the country, the Union of the States, and the
enforcement of the laws'. A few Southern Unionists may have
supported Douglas; a good number must have joined Bell, but
the bulk of the Southerners were behind Breckinridge. Whatever the differences between Southerners, Breckinridge was the
only obvious Southern candidate. Douglas was anathema to
most Southerners for his popular sovereignty doctrine, while
Bell offered no permanent solution but simply a temporary
home for those torn in their loyalty between the Union and the
South.

Well before the election of 1860 Southern politicians and
editorials clearly announced that the election of a Republican
President on the platform of slavery limitation in the territories
would result in Southern secession from the Union. All candi-

[5] Davis introduced resolutions in the Senate during 1860 which
sum up the demands of his party:
  (i) No state had the right to interfere with domestic institu-
      tions of other states.
 (ii) Any attack on slavery within slave states was violation of
      Constitution.
(iii) Congress had no right to limit the right to hold slaves in
      territories and must extend protection to them by means
      of a slave code.
 (iv) Territories could not decide the slavery question until ad-
      mission to the Union.
  (v) Any state legislation interfering with return of fugitive
      slaves was contrary to the spirit of the Constitution.

dates in the South—Douglas, Breckinridge or Bell—whatever their policies, were agreed in either threatening to leave or reserving the right to leave a Union administered by Republicans. Though the Republicans were faced with this mass of evidence of impending catastrophe, they were able to ignore the whole matter. The constantly reiterated threats of secession during the past decades, like the ticking of a familiar clock, had to all intents and purposes ceased to be audible to them. They had heard it too often; they had become agitated too many times and their capacity for alarm was exhausted. They considered it to be pure bluff and in the electoral campaign they scoffed at the idea that it might ever take place. Their attitude was that of a young Republican, Carl Schurz, who said lightheartedly in a speech:

There have been two overt attempts at secession already: one the secession of the southern students from the Medical School at Philadelphia; the second upon the election of Speaker Pennington when the South seceded from Congress, went out, took a drink, and came back. The third attempt will be when Old Abe is elected; they would again secede and this time would take two drinks and come back again.

This refusal to take Southern threats seriously is of vital importance. The voters of the North, many of whom were destined to die in battle, were never confronted with the issue that a Republican President would mean secession. Republicans consistently denied that the threat deserved to be taken seriously. In considering the causes of the Civil War this failure of perception is of tragic importance.

In the South it was by no means simply empty words or bluff. Even if it had been bluff it never follows that if the bluff is called action will not result. A loaded revolver may be used as bluff in a robbery, but there is no guarantee that it will not be fired if the threat itself does not suffice. Three Southern states took formal legislative measures preparatory to action in the event of a Republican victory. The fire-eaters intended to have everything prepared this time, unlike 1850. South Carolina issued a call in which Mississippi joined for a

general convention of slave-holding states to meet in June
1860 to discuss measures in event of a Republican victory.
Alabama, sick of co-operative action, passed a resolution for
a state convention to meet in the event of Lincoln's success.
This conflict between immediate and co-operative action was
important; in it lay the hope of Southern moderates to delay
a show-down and the hope of all those who while approving
of secession in theory were eager to avoid the issue in practice. The story of the secession movement is neither simple nor
clear cut. There was no sweeping Southern movement; action
was piecemeal and in many states the extremists forced a decision without a proper democratic mandate behind them.

On the news of Lincoln's election the South Carolina legislature, which was meeting to choose members of the electoral
college, decided by a unanimous vote to summon a state convention. This met on December 20th and passed without a
dissenting vote the resolution 'that the Union now subsisting
between South Carolina and other states is hereby dissolved'.
The excitement was intense and pandemonium broke out as a
member cried: 'The tea has been thrown overboard; the Revolution of 1860 has begun'. Commissioners were then appointed
to treat with the United States Government about the disposal
of Federal property within the State. South Carolina thus
showed the way. In the other states, however, the moderates
fought a powerful but unco-ordinated rearguard action. Many
pressed for a general convention of the states to draw up
grievances and present them to the Republicans before taking
decisive action. Lonely voices called for patience until a positive act of aggression had been committed by the Republican
administration. Unfortunately, the moderates could not point
to a positive act by Congress or to any positive statement by
Republican leaders which would support their plea for patience. The extremists, on the other hand, could point to past
history and to the recorded statements of Northern politicians.
Often isolated and threatened even by physical violence,
Southern Unionists fought a losing battle. The policy of immediate action won the day and by February 1st, 1861, South
Carolina, Mississippi, Florida, Alabama, Georgia, Louisiana
and Texas had left the Union (the last against the violent op-

position of its famous Governor Sam Houston). The moderates failed too in their final attempt to get the ordinances of secession submitted to the voters for ratification, except in Texas. As one editor said, Southern leaders 'were afraid to trust the second thoughts of their own people'.

Individual studies of the secession movements reveal many intricacies and anomalies—in the selection of delegates, in the method of voting, and in the procedure followed within the convention. In Louisiana and South Carolina, for example, representation depended on the amount of taxation contributed by an area. A referendum held throughout the South would not have altered the verdict (since the voters would have followed their leaders), but it would probably have modified the appearance of unanimity with which the seven states severed their connection with the Union. The extremists had finally won the day, but even among those who had supported them, there were many who hoped that secession would not be permanent, that it would simply enable the South to get better terms from the North before returning to a Union with adequate protection for Southern rights. The active minority succeeded because, as Burke said, 'The great number is generally composed of men of sluggish tempers slow to act and unwilling to attempt, and by being in possession are so disposed to peace that they are unwilling to take early and vigorous measures for their defence'. South Carolina's precipitate haste caught the conservatives unprepared, and once the crisis was on them, social pressure, denunciations and threats of violence cowed the Unionists. They had nothing to offer but moderation, and the failure of Congress to produce any compromise measures when it met in December destroyed any hope of arresting the secession movement in the Lower South. The Unionists had nothing to set against the intoxicating cry of 'States' rights'.

Secession resulted from the logic of the states' rights theory carried into effect under the leadership of the Southern nationalists. Yet the Southern nationalists would hardly have won if other Southern leaders had not believed that the election of a Republican President so threatened their rights as a minority as to justify the ultimate sanction of state sovereignty. There still remains the question of how much reality lay behind these

fears of the Southerners and in what sense the election of a
Republican President justified the extreme course of secession.

There is no doubt that in 1860 the Republican party had
receded from the ultra position it had adopted in 1856. As a
party it was no longer as zealous or as homogeneous as the
crusading band which had sprung up six years before in response to the Kansas-Nebraska Act. Great numbers of old
Whigs and dissatisfied Democrats had joined their ranks, and
many of them were politicians eager for the power and place
of which they had been so long deprived. Thus was a tradition
of compromise and of opportunism joined with the radical fervour which had created the Republican party. At the enthusiastic and confident convention which met at Chicago in May
1860—under a great canvas tent larger than any seen before
—the Radicals had lost the day. The conservative swing gained
Lincoln the nomination instead of Seward. Seward was suspect
as an abolitionist whereas Lincoln was an old-time Whig who
had been described by Garrison as 'the slave hound of Illinois'.
Under such a candidate the Republicans were more likely to
win support in the border states. The Republican platform had
indeed denied the right of slavery to go into the territories
but it had many other planks, such as the tariff and the Homestead Act,[6] designed to appeal to the widest selection of votes.
The allusion to slavery as a relic of barbarism was omitted;
John Brown's raid was referred to as a lawless invasion; and
the rights of states over their domestic institutions were reiterated. This was certainly not a Radical platform, but was it
merely giving the appearance of moderation in order to gain
the victory? It would have been worth while for the South to
wait and see. She still controlled the Supreme Court and the
Senate, while the Republican party appeared to be torn by
dissension and tending towards conservatism. As we shall see,
compromise measures appeared in the House and the Senate
between December 1860 and March 1861; two committees
were also set up to consider the crisis and, on every measure
proposed, a majority of Republicans were in favour of modera-

[6] The Homestead Act was passed in 1862. It offered a citizen or
intending citizen over 21, *or* the head of a family, 160 acres virtually free.

tion. Moreover the figures in the Presidential election had shown that there was no overwhelming majority behind the Republicans. Lincoln had gained 1,866,352 votes to the total vote of the three other candidates of 2,810,051. A considerable number of Northerners, therefore, had not voted Republican. The majority of voters in the nation were not agreed that the containment of slavery was either essential or desirable. The Republicans had won no mandate and with the Supreme Court and the Senate the South possessed constitutional safeguards against a President who had won a minority of national votes and whose party was far from cohesive.

Against this view it could be argued that the Radicals within the Republican party, in a sense, held the balance of power and that, as we shall see, Lincoln always refused to consider compromise on the issue of slavery extension. But he was also to resist firmly all Radical importunities to abolish slavery until he decided that emancipation could be a good weapon with which to win the war. The real point, however, is that the South was in no mood to consider the pros and cons of secession or to assess correctly the reality of the Republican victory. The South collectively had lost its capacity to analyse the situation coolly, and to perceive the potential advantages of playing a waiting game. If Southern leaders had retained enough detachment of mind to weigh the factors involved, they might well have chosen not to inaugurate the programme of secession. But the South in general attempted no analysis: it preferred an emotional stereotype which pictured Lincoln and all his supporters as negrophiles of such extreme fanaticism that they had chosen a mulatto—Hannibal Hamlin—as Vice-President! In the angry mood built up by years of antagonism, the South could not distinguish degrees of hostility to slavery. To many the testing time had come. If they were states' rights men they could not risk the possibilities of the future; for it seemed that the Southern way of life was threatened within a Federal Union where the Northern majority had won power. And to the Southern nationalists here was the opportunity to achieve their secret ambitions.

Yet even with secession, war was not inevitable. Compromise might well come from the North. Many Southerners believed that it would and had supported secession because they felt that being outside the Union they might secure safeguards to return within it. Moreover eight slave states—Delaware, Maryland, Virginia, North Carolina, Kentucky, Tennessee, Missouri and Arkansas—still remained within the Union. Even if secession were not revoked, why should war follow? Surely the North would not attempt to maintain the Union by force. So men argued in one way or the other and the months ahead indeed had infinite possibilities within them. Few men in the autumn of 1860 believed that before a year was out thousands would have died in the bloodiest of civil wars. For secession by itself did not make war inevitable and it remains to consider why war came.

CHAPTER VI

THE CAUSES OF WAR

As we have seen, sectionalism had created antagonisms which had led to the secession of seven Southern states. The situation potentially threatened war but potentialities do not determine events; they only determine the limits within which events occur. War crises have often existed without a war resulting and it is therefore necessary to study the months from December 1860 to April 1861 to see how the war came. Perhaps then we may be better able individually to decide why it came.

It is generally agreed that the interregnum period of four months[1] between succeeding Presidencies was an unhappy provision of the American Constitution. Herbert Hoover in 1932 and James Buchanan in 1860 are the most conspicuous examples of a lame duck President. In a ministerial form of government the new leader would have taken over the reins of government at once. As it was, from November 1860 to March 1861 the Republicans were without responsibility for the government but at the same time they possessed a vast influence over the course of events. The interregnum would not have been so unfortunate if Buchanan's administration had had a decisive policy to meet the crisis or if the Republican party had been united with an acknowledged leader and policy. Neither of these conditions existed until the beginning of January, and then only in part. By then secession was in full flood and the opportunities for negotiation had seriously decreased. Buchanan was an old man, irresolute, inert and prejudiced in favour of the South. Throughout his Presidency

[1] The 20th amendment of the constitution (1933) limited the interregnum to two months.

control of affairs had virtually been in the hands of certain
members of his Cabinet.[2] His Cabinet contained three Southerners who can really be called secessionists: Howell Cobb of
Georgia, the Secretary of the Treasury; John B. Floyd of Virginia, the Secretary of War, and Jacob Thompson of Mississippi, the Secretary of the Interior. Floyd and Thompson were
passionate men of limited ability who early in December 1860
were to be revealed as heavily involved in, though not directly
responsible for, considerable embezzlement of government
funds. The senior member of the Cabinet was Lewis Cass of
Michigan, an aged, gross opportunist whose influence was
quite unable to counterbalance the dominating pressure of the
Southerners on the President. The one bastion for the Union
was Jeremiah Black, the Attorney-General, assisted by Joseph
Holt, the Postmaster-General. Outside the Cabinet, Southern
Congressmen like John Slidell, Jefferson Davis and James
Mason intrigued with the Southerners inside.

At first under this pressure Buchanan appeared as if he
were going to admit the right of secession, and he gave up
his original plan of calling a convention of the States. In his
message to Congress on December 3rd he took up the neutral
position of denying the right of secession but at the same time
denying the right of the government to do anything about it.
This was no policy to prevent secession, and matters were allowed to drift until the question of the Charleston forts brought
things to a head within the Cabinet and caused the withdrawal
of the Southern members.

There were three forts in Charleston harbour: Castle Pinck-
ney with 8 guns and 4 howitzers, Fort Moultrie with 55 guns
and the unfinished Fort Sumter with 78 guns. The total Federal contingent was under the command of Major Anderson,
who had his headquarters at Fort Moultrie. General Winfield
Scott, the aged General-in-Chief known by the nickname of
'Old Fuss and Feathers', advised the President to reinforce
Anderson. The Southerners in the Cabinet objected violently

---

[2] A typical comment by Buchanan when pressed to make a decision: 'You don't give me time to consider; you don't give me time
to say my prayers. I always say my prayers when required to act
on any great state affair.'

and Buchanan unfortunately gave way to them; on December 9th he gave commissioners from South Carolina to understand that he would not alter the *status quo* of the forts without prior warning. South Carolina then started a campaign to have the forts surrendered to the state government. A violent conflict raged in the Cabinet and the climax was reached when news arrived that Anderson had moved his headquarters from Moultrie to the stronger Fort Sumter. Floyd and Thompson insisted that the President should disown Anderson's action which they claimed transgressed the pledge Buchanan had given. Black and Holt said they would resign if the President did give way. On Sunday, December 30th, the crisis came when the President, at last affronted by Southern insults and abuse, wrote an answer to the South Carolina commissioners —'This I cannot do: this I will not do'—and gave orders for a relief fleet to be sent to Charleston. Floyd and Thompson both resigned and an end was written to appeasement. At last the government had a policy but it was too late to stop secession.

It is now time to look at the Republican party and its behaviour in these months of destiny. Its growth since 1856 had not made it a united party; it was a collection of Whigs, Free Soil Democrats, abolitionists, Know Nothings,[3] commanded by professional politicians eager for place and power, so long denied to them by the tenure in office of a Democratic party dominated by Southerners. The Republican platform in 1860[4] had been designed to attract as many votes as possible and, although the abolitionists were vociferous, they were few in number. The voters in 1860 had supported the Republican party for many reasons and very few ever thought of pursuing the anti-slavery cause to the brink of war.

From the moment of victory this motley party produced a discordant chorus of policies to be pursued in face of Southern secession. The hubbub in newspaper editorials, on public

[3] A nation-wide secret society founded in 1849 whose main object was to oppose immigration (particularly the large Catholic immigration from Ireland). The nickname 'Know Nothing' came from the answer made by members of the society to any enquiry about their activities.

[4] See above, p. 92.

platforms, in Congress, in clubs and saloons was tremendous. Basically there were three main policies suggested: 'let them go', which was an unreal policy avoiding the real issue of the extension of slavery; coercion, to force the seceding states back to the Union; or compromise. By far the loudest support was for the last, and enormous pressure came especially from the business interests of the North. On December 15th a meeting of 2,000 merchants in New York supported compromise. In Boston a petition of 14,000 signatures from a total population of 19,000 endorsed the view expressed in the second part of the question: 'Shall we stand upon a platform made some time ago in view of facts which then existed and which have ceased to exist now; or shall we be willing to yield some fair concession without any sacrifice of principle?' The Whig party's tradition of compromise supported this view, but the decision as to the policy to be followed obviously lay with the leader of the party. But who was the leader? Lincoln, the President-elect, was an unknown and uncouth Whig who had only received national notice by his debates with Douglas in 1858 and by his tour of the East in the spring of 1860. His nomination at the Chicago convention had come as a shock to many Republicans, particularly to the accepted leader of the party, William H. Seward of New York, and his manager, Thurlow Weed, the Albany editor and political boss of New York state.

Seward was a man of remarkable appearance and superb political talents. A hook nose, receding chin and large ears made his face memorable and he was renowned for taking snuff and flourishing a large yellow handkerchief. He was exceedingly sociable and had been well known as a Whig senator for many years. As the author of the phrase 'the irrepressible conflict', he had come to represent to the South the anti-slavery cause in the Senate. He had been groomed by Thurlow Weed as destined for the White House and there was no political boss shrewder than this tall, handsome intriguer from Albany. 'Know him?', Weed is reputed to have said of some politician pointed out to him, 'I created him'. He had dissuaded Seward from seeking the Republican nomination in 1856 because he recognized that the time was not yet ripe for a Republican victory. But in 1860 he expected success and at Seward's home

1 Auburn he and the candidate sat waiting confidently with annon prepared to announce the news of victory when it arived. On the first ballot at the convention Seward had 173½ otes to Lincoln's 102; on the second, Seward 184½ and Linoln 181. The third ballot lost Seward the nomination with 80 votes to Lincoln's 231½; this caused five Ohio delegates 3 change their votes and Lincoln passed the 234 vote limit eeded for the nomination.

The reasons for Seward's defeat were primarily that he ained the support of neither Pennsylvania nor Indiana. To Republican bosses, like Simon Cameron[5] of Pennsylvania, eward was not only personally distasteful but was, in their pinion, too closely identified with the anti-slavery cause to 'in votes from the Border states. The bargains made by Linoln's campaign managers without his authority were really nnecessary; neither Indiana nor Pennsylvania would have upported Seward. As it was, both Cameron and Caleb B. mith of Indiana gained promises of Cabinet office in return or throwing their states into Lincoln's camp.

Seward heard the news with an ashen face and Weed burst nto tears. The blow was a shattering one but when they reovered it seemed possible to retrieve something from the uins of their hopes. Who, after all, was this unknown man rom Illinois? It would surely be possible to ignore him and or Seward to dictate policy as the true leader of the Repubican party. For only one man outside Illinois had sized Linoln up and reached a verdict with which most historians toay would agree. This man was Gideon Welles, an austere, ilent Democrat from Connecticut. In due course he was to oin Lincoln's Cabinet as Secretary of the Navy and his tall, earded figure lends a patriarchal dignity to the pictures of he Republican Cabinet. The diary he kept throughout the 'ar provides a fascinating insight into the workings of Civil

[5] Cameron's quality as a politician can be seen in these two necdotes. When asked to describe an honest politician he replied:)ne when bought, stays bought'. Thaddeus Stevens when asked y Lincoln if Cameron was an honest man, replied: 'He would not :eal a red hot stove'. On being challenged over this later, he relied: 'Oh, well, I apologise. I said Cameron would not steal a red ot stove. I withdraw that statement.'

War politics and from the beginning he recognized the quality
of Lincoln.

> This orator and lawyer has been caricatured. He is not
> Apollo but he is not Caliban. He was made where the
> material for strong men is plenty; and his loose tall frame
> is loosely thrown together. He is in every way large, brain
> included, but his countenance shows intellect, generosity,
> great good nature and keen discrimination. . . . He is an
> effective speaker because he is earnest, strong, honest,
> simple in style and clear as crystal in his logic.

To Seward and Weed, however, Lincoln was a nonentity
and their conduct until January 1861, and in many respect
until April, was based on this judgement. Over policy and
Cabinet making, they regarded the Republican victory o
1860 as the resurrection of the old Whig party, whose forme
members had provided the majority of Lincoln's votes: th
coming administration was to be a Whig administration unde
Seward. It is a revealing commentary on this attitude that Lin
coln on the eve of the Inaugural Ball in April said to a reporte
from New York who asked him for a statement: 'You may tel
your Editor that Thurlow Weed has discovered that Sewar
was not nominated at Chicago'.

Seward's assumption that he was still the leader of the part
was made possible because Lincoln at Springfield preserve
an obstinate silence both during the campaign and after hi
election. Although thousands of people descended on the smal
capital of Illinois to be shown into Lincoln's small house, t
sit on horse-hair sofas and drink Mrs. Lincoln's homemade bev
erages, there were no announcements of policy to be heard
Lincoln's silence was deliberate. He felt that sectional antago
nism fed upon discussion. His own position and views had
been stated and could be read in his speeches. By remaining
silent now he could avoid any attempt to bully him into modi
fying his platform. To him the election of 1860 was a turning
point in American history: a national crisis had called into ex
istence a new party of which he was the head. The voters had
made him President and he intended to accept the trust and

he responsibility. Naturally he wanted Seward in his Cabinet
but he intended it to be on his terms, not Seward's.

This was the background of the struggle for power within
the Republican party in the autumn and winter of 1860–61.
The struggle itself centred on both policy and the choice of
Cabinet officers. Compromise was the heart of the Whig tradition and on November 24th Weed's paper *The Albany Evening
Journal* carried an editorial suggesting that a restoration of the
Missouri Compromise line would be the basis for a compromise
settlement with the South. During December Senator John J.
Crittenden of Kentucky introduced a resolution in the Senate
which would have recognized slavery south of the line 36° 30′
and have all the peripheral issues embodied in unamendable
amendments to the constitution. In face of these moves Lincoln broke his silence by sending a letter to Senator Lyman
Trumbull, a former Free Soiler. This was intended to arrest
the growing move for compromise in Congress. He stated his
case plainly:

> Let there be no compromise on the question of extend-
> ing slavery. If there be, all our labour is lost and ere long
> must be done again. The dangerous ground, that into
> which some of our friends have a hankering to run is
> popular sovereignty. Have none of it. Stand firm. The tug
> has to come and better now than at any time thereafter.

He believed that the election of 1860 had been a positive vote
that slavery on no account must be extended. It could remain
where it already existed but the South must be told without
prevarication 'Thus far and no further'.

This move in policy by Lincoln was connected with his desire to win Seward to his side, on his terms, so that Seward
could be the Republican spokesman in Congress until the new
administration was in office. On December 17th Weed received
an invitation to visit Springfield. He went in high hopes but
came away having learnt the lesson that Lincoln had a mind
of his own. He was irritated by the President-elect's prairie
anecdotes and gained no satisfaction over policy or the Cabinet. Lincoln made clear that his Cabinet was to be a balanced
Unionist one containing three Whigs and four Democrats, one

of whom, Salmon P. Chase of Ohio, was particularly distasteful to the Seward group. On policy Lincoln declared firmly
that he was opposed to compromise and gave Weed certain
resolutions for Seward to introduce in Congress. On December
21st Seward joined Weed's train at Syracuse and received a
report of his manager's interview with Lincoln. The next day
he made a speech at the Astor House in New York in which
no mention of compromise appeared. Three days later in
Washington he introduced certain resolutions in the Senate
Committee of thirteen which virtually killed the Crittenden
compromise. On December 28th he wrote to Lincoln accepting
the office of Secretary of State. It appeared as if the Republican party was at length united behind a policy and a leader
at the same time as the Buchanan administration was being
reorganized.

Seward indeed became the spokesman of Republican policy
for the next two months but at heart he remained uncon-
verted. He still believed he was the most important man in the
party on whom the salvation of the country depended. 'The
present administration and the incoming are united in devolv-
ing on me the responsibility of diverting these disasters.' He
believed too that the policy he pursued was fundamentally his
own and at bottom he was still prepared to compromise to
avert war. He so utterly misjudged Lincoln that he was able
to send the President an astonishing document on April 1st,
accusing him of having no policy: 'Either the President must
do it himself or devolve it on some member of the Cabinet. It
is not my special province but I neither seek to evade or assume responsibility.'

Yet superficially it is true that Seward's and Lincoln's policies were basically similar from the beginning of January. Both
men suffered from two great illusions. The first was that the
secession movement was not serious, and the second that
Southern Unionism was extremely strong. There was a certain
truth in both these assumptions but it was highly dangerous to
base a policy on them. Granted these beliefs, the rejection of
compromise by Lincoln (and apparently by Seward) did not
mean that their alternative policy was war. Theirs was a third
solution: the peaceful and voluntary reconstruction of the

Union, once Southern Unionist feeling had reasserted itself and shown secession to be a conspiracy led by minority groups of hotheads. For the success of this policy it was vital to retain the loyalty of the Border states. If this area could be kept loyal to the Union, the Confederacy of seven states was almost laughable. Unionist sentiment would have little difficulty in ultimately bringing these seven states back to the Union. So Republican policy from January was clear: no appeasement of the South (for that would only encourage the secessionists) but conciliation, and at all costs retention of the Border states. Armed conflict must be avoided, any assistance to the South from the Buchanan administration must be prevented and above all the authority of the national government must be maintained and respected.

It was to secure the adoption of these policies that Seward devoted himself with enthusiasm and confidence in the months from January to March. The prospects appeared promising. The Confederate Cabinet appointed by Jefferson Davis was conspicuously lacking in Southern fire-eaters. Leading Southerners urged that the door to reunion should be left open and indeed it is true that many Southerners who had voted for secession did so, believing that the South could gain better safeguards by negotiation outside the Union rather than within it. If time could be gained all might yet be saved. Seward's activities and influence were widespread. He was in close touch with Edwin M. Stanton, Buchanan's Attorney-General after Black became Secretary of State; he received assurances from General Scott, the General-in-Chief, that the army was ready to preserve order and prevent any conspiracy against the new administration on March 4th. In both Houses of Congress he worked hard to prevent any hostile legislation against the South being brought to the vote and he maintained close relations with Senators Douglas and Crittenden, both of whom continued to work for peace. When Dakota, Colorado and Nevada were organized as territories it was Seward's influence which saw to it that no mention of slavery was made. To all men, whether Republican zealots, South Carolina commissioners or Border Senators, he had a soothing word to say. He welcomed the Washington Peace Conference called by Vir-

ginia while at the same time he made conciliatory remarks
about the forts in Charleston harbour. Anything in fact which
would allow time for the Unionist reaction to set in was done.
And it seemed as if the policy was succeeding. By the end
of February, Virginia, Tennessee, Arkansas, Missouri and
North Carolina had turned down the proposals for secession
raised in their specially called state conventions. All five states,
however, added the rider that secession would come if force
were used against the seven seceded states. Maryland's Governor and the Kentucky legislature had both refused to call a
convention to discuss the subject of secession.

Thus by March 4th when the Republican administration
entered office, Lincoln's policy, brilliantly executed by Seward,
had succeeded in keeping peace and in maintaining the *status
quo* after the initial secession of the Lower South. Now he was
in power the President could continue this policy personally
and in his Inaugural Speech he elaborated its details. Assert-
ing that the Union was unbroken and that Federal authority
would be maintained, he gave assurance that Federal authority would not impose itself. 'While the strict legal right
may exist in the Government to enforce the exercise of these
offices,[6] the attempt to do so would be so irritating and so
nearly impracticable withal, that I deem it better to forego for
the time the uses of such offices.' At the same time, Federal
property like forts and arsenals would continue to be maintained. 'In your hands, my dissatisfied fellow-countrymen', he
concluded, 'and not in mine is the momentous issue of civil
war. The government will not assail you.'

If the situation could remain thus, the potentialities for
peace might outweigh those for war. Seven seceded states
separated from the North by the solid mass of Border states
were hardly in a position to wage war. Given time and the
calming influence of Unionist sentiment in the Border states,
a settlement might well be reached. But unfortunately Fort
Sumter in the vital state of South Carolina, which had led the
secession movement, presented an issue which did not allow
of time. A certain stability in the situation had been reached

[6] Collection of revenue at ports, delivery of mails and the authority of Federal judges and marshals.

under Buchanan, but on February 28th Major Anderson wrote
to the Commander-in-Chief indicating that he would be unable to hold out for longer than six weeks unless he had more
supplies. As the Charleston authorities refused to have any
relations with Anderson these supplies could only come from
the North. Anderson's note was handed to Lincoln on March
5th and the final crisis had begun.

Over the question of Sumter there are endless complexities
and in assessing the final cause of war it is necessary to consider some of them. Lincoln appeared at first to hesitate and
by the middle of March Seward and the majority of the Cabinet recommended that Sumter should be given up. This was
certainly Seward's policy and in the first month of Lincoln's
administration, when he was at last finding out that the President and not himself was in command, he rashly assured the
Confederate commissioners that Sumter would be surrendered.
Yet Lincoln's apparent hesitation was not hesitation on the
principle of maintaining Federal authority. He was adamant
that the new Republican administration could not afford to
surrender Federal authority in such a symbolic manner. All
very well for Buchanan to sit on the fence, but if he did like-
wise it would be disastrous to the Unionist cause in both the
North and the South. But for all that, he would be prepared
to surrender Sumter if the principle could be asserted in some
other way in a less explosive part of the country than Charleston. His hesitation in fact merely covered his attempts to find
some other means. He offered the help of United States troops
to the Unionist Governor of Texas, Sam Houston, in an attempt
to rally Texas to the Union. He sent an agent to South Carolina
to investigate the situation there. But his most hopeful move
was his desire to reinforce Fort Pickens outside Pensacola in
Florida. On March 5th he mentioned to General Scott that this
fort should be reinforced. Troops were already there aboard
ships sent by Buchanan, but they had never landed in view
of an informal agreement made with the Confederacy. Not
until March 12th did General Scott despatch a message by
sea for the troops to be landed. The message took nineteen
days to arrive and the Naval Commander showed unfortunate
scruples by refusing to obey the order since General Scott was

not in command of the Navy. This refusal was sent by rail through a special courier on April 1st. He arrived in Washington late on April 5th and the next day orders were sent by the Secretary of the Navy for the troops to be landed. On April 12th they did so without any trouble, but by then it was too late, for at 4.30 a.m. that morning the shore batteries at Charleston had opened fire on Fort Sumter.

It is difficult not to feel that here a real chance was lost. A greater sense of urgency, travel by rail instead of sea for the original message, a less scrupulous sense of discipline—any of these might have allowed Pickens to be reinforced much earlier. Yet it would be wrong to give too much weight to this, for in the last half of March opinion had been hardening in the North, that Sumter must be retained. At a Cabinet meeting on March 29th, a remarkable change was seen since only Seward and Caleb Smith still advised evacuation. On the same day Lincoln ordered an expedition to be prepared. On April 4th he sent a message to Anderson that the expedition would go forward. On April 6th, having heard the news from Fort Pickens, he informed the Governor of South Carolina by personal messenger that an attempt would be made to land *provisions only* on Sumter; no men or arms would be landed unless resistance was encountered.

Lincoln did not believe that this attempt to land provisions would necessarily mean war. It was no more than Buchanan had done in January. Yet January was not April and Lincoln was a Republican President. If Sumter was a symbol of Union firmness to many Republicans it had also become to the Southern Confederacy a symbol of their independence and of the right of secession. However much many Southerners thought in terms of reconstructing the Union, it was to be a reconstruction for the better protection of states' rights; to them Sumter was a symbol of the sovereignty of each state which involved the right of secession. To the fire-eaters in Charleston the sight of the Union flag flying over Sumter was intolerable. In this context statesmanship was now powerless to avoid war. On hearing that an attempt to provision Sumter was to be made, the Confederate Cabinet sitting in Montgomery decided with a certain reluctance to order General Beauregard, commanding Confederate troops in Charleston, to summon Anderson to surrender at once. This summons was made on April 11th and rejected. At dawn the next day the guns opened fire.

Once the guns had fired the reaction in both the North and South showed that tension had been at breaking point. The news was followed by Lincoln's call on the 15th for 75,000 volunteers to repress the insurrection. This call drove the four Border states of Virginia, Arkansas, Tennessee and North Carolina into secession. Delaware, Maryland, Kentucky and Missouri remained loyal to the Union but not without prolonged internal quarrels between Unionists and secessionists.

The conflict of loyalties for many individuals was decided by the decision of their states. Yet if the majority of men knew what they had to do, it was not easy for many families in the Border states. Families were often split: Lincoln's Attorney-General, Edward Bates of Maryland, had a son in the Confederate army; Lincoln's wife had a brother, three half-brothers and three brothers-in-law in Confederate ranks; Senator Crittenden of Kentucky had sons in both armies. The examples can be multiplied down to the humblest families. For the majority, however, it was easy. A wave of enthusiasm swept the North and the South now that the years of debate and quarrelling had ended in war. Just as many Britishers were relieved in their hearts in 1939 when Hitler's invasion of Poland put an end to doubts and shame, so in 1861 Sumter did the same for many Americans. Reason and good sense could have prevented war; instead the extremists on both sides had directed the course of events. In the long crisis men were glad that at last some decision had been taken. On neither side did men think of the war as entailing a long and bloody struggle. In the South men flocked with gladness in their hearts to join hastily formed regiments with colourful names such as Tigers, Lions, Scorpions, Palmetto Eagles. Romance and glory seemed to be beckoning. The war would be short: the North would soon realize that it could not conquer the South and, if there were any doubt, foreign aid would speedily secure the independence of the Southern nation. The spirit of reckless enthusiasm has been well portrayed by William Howard Russell, *The*

Times correspondent who visited Charleston a week after the attack on Fort Sumter. He visited the island itself where he found Louis T. Wigfall, a senator from Texas, one of the real fire-eaters from the South. 'If you look some day when the sun is not too bright into the eye of the Bengal Tiger, in the Regent's Park . . . you will form some notion of the expression I mean. It was flashing, fierce yet calm—with a well of fire burning behind and spouting through it, an eye pitiless in anger.' On another island in the harbour he found:

> life and excitement. Officers were galloping about as if on a field day or in action. Commissariat carts were toiling to and fro between the beach and the camps, and sounds of laughter and revelling came from the tents. . . . In every tent was hospitality and a hearty welcome to all comers. Cases of champagne and claret, French pâtés, and the like, were piled outside the canvas walls when there was no room for them inside. In the middle of these excited gatherings I felt like a man in the full possession of his senses coming in late to a wine party.

A party indeed, for few imagined the four years of horror ahead; the 111,000 Northern deaths in battle, the Confederate 94,000 and more than double this number on each side from disease and wounds. The filth, the wounds and the disease were soon to remove the glamour of war.

Lincoln's decision to send a relief expedition to Fort Sumter was the immediate cause of war. The question must be asked 'Was he right to take that decision?' It can be argued that his policy of relying on Union sentiment demanded a policy of caution and waiting. But there comes a time in the affairs of men when to continue conciliation for hopes of future peace becomes a weakness and not a strength. By April 1861 it was Lincoln's belief that a surrender of Sumter would be a disaster to the cause of the Union in both the North and the South. In that sense war became inevitable when Lincoln had come to that conclusion. It was not inevitable before then and Lincoln did not intend to initiate war by ordering the relief expedition to Sumter. But he realized the risk involved and was prepared to accept the decision of events. His own words in his Second Inaugural Address probably sum up the best historical conclusion about the inevitability of war. 'Both parties deprecated war, but one of them would make war rather than let the nation survive, and the other would accept war rather than let it perish. And the war came.' Statesmanship had done its best and its worst. A stand had to be made and Lincoln had the courage to make that stand. It was an individual decision and one for which he was prepared to take an individual responsibility.

CHAPTER VII

THE WAR FROM THE NORTHERN VIEWPOINT

The disastrous battle of First Bull Run in July 1861, when the citizens of Washington watched the stampede of the Northern Army back into the city, made Northerners realize that the war was not to be a short and easy one. The battle was the result of pressure from politicians and the Press to see some action. The raw Union recruits were sent into battle insufficiently trained and, despite initial success, they panicked in face of the Confederate stand made by General T. J. Jackson, who thus gained his nickname 'Stonewall'. This victory for a time confirmed Southern confidence that the Yankees could not fight and that Southern independence was assured. It was only when they failed to gain European recognition and assistance that the South began to understand that the struggle for independence would be hard and long, demanding the last ounce of self-sacrifice from each individual.

Today many historians take the view that the South was doomed from the start. A North of twenty-two million people with strong industrial and railroad developments and all the resources of established government was bound to overwhelm an agricultural country of nine million[1] with inadequate railroads and a makeshift administration. At the time, however, European observers held exactly the opposite view: that the North was inevitably destined to defeat. Despite its greater resources it was felt that the task it had undertaken of conquering the eleven seceded states was far beyond those resources. So widespread was this opinion that it coloured European diplomacy towards the struggle in America. That such a view existed required a reconsideration of the inevitability of North-

[1] 3,500,000 of these were Negroes.

ern success. It could be asked if the South did not rather lose
the war than the North win it. These questions lead straight to
the heart of the matter. As far as historical certainty goes, it
would be true to say that without Lincoln the North would
have given up the struggle. It is easy to forget, in the halo
which surrounded Lincoln from the moment of his assassination, that throughout his Presidency he was regarded by the
majority of Northern political leaders as incompetent for his
office.[2] A member of the Republican party in Illinois wrote in
early 1862: 'We are nearly paralyzed by the imbecility of
President Lincoln in the management of the war'. The Secretary of the Treasury felt: 'We are in a deplorable condition;
armies inactive, councils uncertain, credit drooping'. 'Public
opinion is deep and bitter against Mr. Lincoln because he is
looked upon as an obstacle in the way of closing up this war
. . .', wrote one radical: another held the view that Lincoln
was 'as near lunacy as anyone not a pronounced Bedlamite'.
In 1862 the mid-term Congressional elections showed a marked
trend against the administration, and when 1864 came with
its Presidential election, few believed that Lincoln could be re-
elected. 'President Lincoln is a joke incarnate', remarked the
editor of a New York paper. 'His election was a very sorry
joke . . . his intrigues and the hopes he entertains for a re-
election are however the most laughable jokes of all.' Lincoln
himself was almost resigned to defeat in 1864 and even after
his nomination was faced by a strong Republican demand that
he should withdraw before the election.

Yet just as historical and contemporary opinions have differed over the likely outcome of the war, so have they differed
in their judgement of Lincoln. It has become increasingly the
opinion of historians that the survival of the Union was primarily due to Lincoln. To examine the war from the Northern
viewpoint it is therefore necessary to examine this opinion.

Lincoln had already shown the hard core of his determination in the months between election and inauguration. His was
a character which few of his contemporaries understood while
even fewer of them recognized the firmness of purpose underlying all his actions. His frontier humour they mistook for rus-

[2] See J. G. Randall, *The Unpopular Mr. Lincoln*.

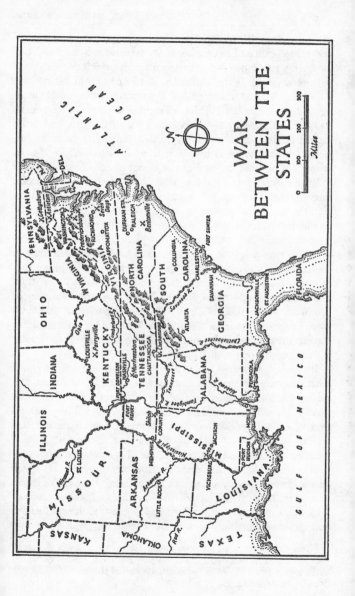

tic uncertainty; his physical gaucheness for political ineptitude, and his tolerance of impertinence for weakness. Yet behind his outward appearance there lay an unbending spirit dedicated to the preservation of the Union by all means within his power, whatever the cost might be to his personal feelings and prestige. General George B. McClellan, the arrogant young commander of the Army of the Potomac after Bull Run, had little regard for his official chief. He mistook Lincoln's humility for weakness and wrote to his wife: 'I went to the White House where I found the original gorilla about as intelligent as ever. What a specimen to be at the head of our affairs now.' Lincoln knew of this contempt but because he believed that McClellan was the best of Northern generals then available, he said: 'I would hold McClellan's horse for him if that would help to win the war'. This surrender of his personal feelings was the price he was prepared to pay to carry out his overriding responsibility for preserving the Union. To this end he submitted to every kind of studied insult; he tolerated disloyalty within the Cabinet simply because he believed the individuals composing it were excellent heads of their departments; he humoured opposition from all quarters, keeping his policies flexible, and many times showing that he was a more skilful politician than his opponents.

By the American Constitution the President is entrusted with supreme authority as Commander-in-Chief of the armed forces. Lincoln appreciated that the war involved both a military and a political problem. In a sense every military operation was also a police one since it was a war to restore the Union. It was not a war to destroy slavery, though ultimately Lincoln was prepared to emancipate the slaves in rebel territory as a weapon of war.[3] The military problem by itself was a gigantic one, for the task of subduing the Confederacy was formidable. Yet Lincoln from the beginning had a clear idea of his intentions. It is never easy to unravel the confusions and muddles which are an inherent part of any war. Aims and

---

[3] The Emancipation Proclamation of January 1st, 1863, declared that all slaves in areas still in rebellion were 'then, thence forward, and forever free'. It did not emancipate slaves in areas already under Federal control.

intentions are modified or distorted by circumstances, by chance and by external pressure. Lincoln, more than any Commander-in-Chief, was subject to pressure, but broadly speaking his plans for winning the war were clear.

Bearing always in mind that his primary aim was to reconstruct the Union, he made it his first concern to retain the loyalty of the remaining Border states (Maryland, Kentucky, Missouri) by sending Federal troops to their support. His next object was to regain Tennessee and thus encourage Unionist sentiment in the South, while at the same time providing a base aimed at the heart of the Confederacy. Thirdly, he intended to blockade the South thus cutting off its opportunity of buying munitions of war from Europe. Fourthly, he planned to cut the Confederacy in two by gaining control of the whole Mississippi; this plan was successful when Vicksburg fell on July 4th, 1863. New Orleans had been captured by Federal troops over a year before in April 1862. Finally there was the Eastern theatre of operations between the two capitals, Washington and Richmond. The most famous Civil War battles[4] were fought in this area between the Army of the Potomac and the Army of Northern Virginia. Both armies were seeking to capture the other's capital; if either had succeeded it would have been of profound moral importance. If Washington had fallen at any time the Northern will to victory would have collapsed, and Lincoln realized this. He also recognized that the destruction of Lee's army, even more than the capture of Richmond, would have a similar effect on the Confederacy. Washington indeed was threatened more than once and Richmond finally fell in the closing weeks of the war. During the four years of war this area of Virginia between the Potomac and James rivers saw the grave of many thousands of men and many military reputations. General Robert E. Lee alone emerged with an immortal name and he was vanquished, not so much by the last commander of the Federal Army, General Ulysses S. Grant, as by the patient determination of the President, Lincoln. Despite heart-breaking failures and disappointments Lincoln persisted in his intention of destroying the

[4] Antietam 1862, Fredericksburg 1862, Chancellorsville 1863, Gettysburg 1863 (in Pennsylvania), Battle of the Wilderness 1864.

Confederate army. General after general failed in the task but the will to victory remained with the Commander-in-Chief.

These then were Lincoln's broad aims of policy in waging the war, but the obstacles in the way of achieving them were enormous. In the first place the United States Army was virtually non-existent. In 1861 the military resources consisted of 15,000 professional troops scattered throughout the continent in remote posts. The South had always supplied a majority of officers for the army and on secession many of them resigned their commissions and joined the Confederacy.[5] No general staff, no plans for war and no maps existed. There was no experience available for war on the scale envisaged by Lincoln; the Mexican war of 1848 had been fought with a total force of 10,000 men, mainly in relatively minor engagements.

In fact the Federal Army had to be recruited from scratch. Lincoln's initial call had been for 75,000 volunteers to serve for three months. This state militia was plainly inadequate: poorly trained and often incompetently officered by men appointed for political reasons or elected by the troops, it could not meet the needs of the time. The term of enlistment was soon lengthened and in March 1863 a Conscription Act made all men between 20 and 45 liable to military service. Exemption was relatively easy to obtain on payment and in practice the bulk of the Federal armies was recruited from volunteers. In all over one and a half million men enlisted in the four years of war for an average period of three years.

This massive army had to be equipped and trained. In 1861 there was no industrial machine capable of providing for such a host, and the taxation system of the United States was wholly inadequate to finance it. In all these matters, therefore, there had to be a revolutionary expansion. For political reasons which will be dealt with later, Lincoln was compelled to take the initiative by using his powers as President. His actions laid him open to the charge of acting unconstitutionally and his political enemies were not slow to accuse him. Lincoln un-

[5] Lincoln offered Robert E. Lee of Virginia command of the Union armies in April 1861. He refused and resigned on the grounds that 'with all my devotion to the Union and the feeling of loyalty and duty of an American citizen, I have not been able to make up my mind to raise my hand against my relatives, my children, my home'.

doubtedly used Presidential powers in an entirely novel way, but realized that the situation required it. War demands quick action, and the constitutional procedures of Congress and the law courts were slow. Lincoln was prepared to act and ask permission afterwards; he called out volunteers on his own authority, he spent money before Congress had appropriated it and he suspended Habeas Corpus in areas where Confederate sympathies were strong. In all these matters he acted swiftly and whatever his Radical opponents in Congress might say at the time, he did so in the interests of waging the war. In time of war constitutional safeguards are necessarily weakened and under Lincoln 'the constitution was stretched but not subverted'.

The administrative genius in the task of equipping the army was Edwin M. Stanton. He was appointed Secretary of War in January 1862 in place of Simon Cameron, the corrupt political boss of Pennsylvania. Cameron had been given the office as a reward for bringing the Pennsylvanian delegation to Lincoln's support at the nominating Convention. His tenure of the office was marked by corruption and incompetence. Stanton on the other hand was hard and ruthless, and can be counted as one of the great war ministers of history. He was an egoist consumed with energy and ambition and a weaker man than Lincoln would have found it difficult to control him. As it was, Lincoln harnessed his energy to the war effort and the ultimate Union success owes much to Stanton's burning vitality. At times his vanity was intolerable but Lincoln humoured him, bore with him and used him in the interests of victory. No Union Army was short of men, ammunition or equipment if Stanton could avoid it.

Quite apart from making and equipping an army, Lincoln had also to find the generals to lead it. Here unavoidably political considerations had to play a part since Lincoln above all else wished to unite the North behind the cause of Union. Prominent politicians appeared to think that they were capable of being generals or colonels and the President was besieged by offers from all parts of the country. Not only did different states have to be recognized but also different national groups and in the midst of the early pressure Lincoln ruefully remarked: 'There has got to be something done unquestionably in the interest of the Dutch, and to that end I want Schimmelfenning appointed'. Three eminent Democratic politicians became generals—Banks, McClernand and Butler—and all of them were militarily a disaster. But in the interests of unity it was impossible for Lincoln to do otherwise.

Lincoln's relations with his generals have excited more controversy than almost any other subject. The Army never takes kindly to interference from politicians. Readers of Lord Alanbrooke's diaries will recall the aggravation caused to the Chiefs of Staff by Mr. Churchill's intervention in the sphere of strategy and at times even of tactics. Lincoln as President was also Commander-in-Chief and had a constitutional responsibility for the direction of the war. The charge made against him is that he interfered so much that the generals were unable to win the war, as they would have done given a free hand. This charge cannot be substantiated. He certainly did interfere as Commander-in-Chief but in no sense of dictation. As he once wrote to McClellan, 'I do not intend this to be an order in any sense but merely . . . to show you the grounds of my anxiety'. He was quite willing to give full power of directing strategy to any general who showed himself capable of exercising this responsibility. But until he put General Grant in command in 1864 he could find no general sufficiently capable. Where he asked for decision, action, fighting and victory, his generals on the whole gave him hesitation, procrastination, excuses and defeat. Lincoln stuck to McClellan for a long time because he believed that he was fundamentally a good general. He undoubtedly was and rendered a great service to the Union cause by training the Army of the Potomac after First Bull Run. But McClellan possessed a vivid imagination which multiplied the numbers of the enemy to gigantic proportions. He was not prepared to move until he had a sufficient preponderance of men and material and the result was that time after time the opportunity for successful action was lost owing to over-caution.[6] Lincoln realized that McClellan's weakness was his refusal to take action, and his rôle as Commander-in-Chief was

[6] See particularly the campaigns of March to July 1862 around the rivers of Virginia. In early March McClellan only advanced on Manassas after the Confederates had withdrawn.

to prod his reluctant subordinate. The wait before Yorktown in April 1862 brought this letter from the President: 'The present hesitation to move upon an entrenched position is but the story of Manassas repeated: You must act'. Or on another occasion when Lincoln was frustrated by an interminable delay as McClellan piled up impedimenta, he commented sarcastically: 'If at any time you feel able to take the offensive you are not restrained from doing so'. Or again in the autumn of 1862 after Antietam where McClellan had gained a technical victory by forcing Lee to withdraw back into Virginia, Lincoln burst out in complaint at McClellan's immobility: 'I have just read your despatches about sore tongued and fatigued horses. Will you pardon me for asking what the horses of your army have done since the battle of Antietam that fatigues anything?' Lee's invasion of Maryland in 1862 and of Pennsylvania in 1863 were both baulked, the former at Antietam, the latter by General Meade at Gettysburg. Both times the Northern generals were too timid, too cautious or too overawed by their opponent Lee to take advantage of their success. When Lincoln dismissed McClellan in November 1862 he commented to a veteran politician: 'He has got the slows, Mr. Blair. He is an admirable engineer but he seems to have a special talent for a stationary engine.'

There is something to be said on both sides. A politician is subject to pressures from his party, the public and the Press. He wishes to see victory and is liable to close his eyes to the problems of training, equipment and administration.[7] He has to assess the will to victory on the home front and believes that war, like politics, is often the art of the possible. Most generals, on the other hand, do not wish to take risks; they wish to prepare as far as humanly possible for all eventualities and would prefer to lose some element of surprise and speed if it means that their men are better trained and equipped. Some generals are lucky but it is not a factor to count upon and the majority of them prefer to be careful. McClellan was justified

[7] See John Connell, *Auchinleck*, for exchanges of letters in the Second World War between Mr. Churchill and Field Marshal Auchinleck which illustrate the two points of view—that of the general in the field and the politician.

in not wishing to overstrain the untrained armies of the North in the early months of the war, but on balance Lincoln was right in trying to make him take action. The North needed a victory. Already Lincoln had seen the quality he was looking for in his generals. In April 1862 General Grant had won a great and bloody victory at Shiloh in Tennessee; 13,000 Union troops were lost compared with 11,000 Confederates, but the Confederates had to withdraw to Corinth in Mississippi. Grant had, however, shown a willingness to fight and when Lincoln received complaints of Grant's drunkenness, he replied: 'I can't spare this man, he fights'. He further enquired the name of Grant's brand of whisky, saying he wished to send a barrel of it to his other generals.

But before Grant was appointed to supreme command of the Union armies two long and costly years of disappointment and disaster were to come. In July 1862 Lincoln had appointed Major-General Halleck as General-in-Chief of the United States armies in an attempt to co-ordinate the Union military effort. In effect Halleck was to be a Chief of the General Staff, and the experiment might have worked if Halleck had been a more sympathetic and imaginative man. As it was he was resented by the generals in the field. Known as 'Old Brains', he was a man of great ability with degrees in engineering, law and military science. He liked everything to be precise, hating waste and disorder. As an administrator he gave great service but Lincoln was still compelled to give a personal direction to the war which has earned him much criticism. In November he finally decided to get rid of McClellan, and command was given to General Ambrose Burnside, who was replaced after the shattering disaster of Fredericksburg (13th December). His reluctance to accept command with the words, 'I do not want the command. I am not competent to command such a large army', had really been fully justified. His successor was General Joseph Hooker, a brave, vain man whose main fault was over-confidence and an inability to keep his plans flexible. He was strongly supported in the Cabinet by Salmon P. Chase and in the Congress by the Radical leaders. Lincoln sought to give guidance and help to Hooker. 'Have you already in mind a plan?' he wrote. 'If you have, prosecute it without interference from me. If you have not, please inform me, so that I, incompetent as I may be, can try and assist in the formation of some plan for the army.' This was typical of the quality of Lincoln's interference—modest, constant and firm.

Hooker fought the battle of Chancellorsville in early May, 1863, with 130,000 men to Lee's 60,000. It was the South's costliest victory both in men killed and through the death of Stonewall Jackson, to whose loss can probably be attributed Lee's failure at Gettysburg in July. Chancellorsville had the effect of shaking Hooker's nerve to such an extent that he appeared incapable of making any plans. To get rid of him would have profoundly affected Northern morale particularly since he retained the solid support of his friends in Congress. As Lee began the preparations for the Gettysburg campaign Hooker deluged Washington with complaints of his difficulties and in a fit of temper wrote an impetuous note: 'I must have more men. This is my resignation else.' Lincoln, advised by Halleck, accepted it as such and appointed General George Meade to take command. This was on June 28th and Gettysburg was fought on 1st–3rd July.

This great battle was the result of Lee's plan to carry the war into the North and it marked the high tide of the South. No battle in the Civil War is more memorable and the full account of it should be read in D. S. Freeman, *R. E. Lee*. The climax came on the afternoon of July 3rd when Lee launched the famous charge of Pickett's division against the Union centre, which he mistakenly believed to be the weakest point of the enemy line. Pickett's charge can be said to symbolize all the courage and chivalry of the South. As three long grey lines of Confederate soldiers advanced up to Cemetery Ridge they were hurled back in a hail of fire. The advance continued but in the end less than half a company reached the objective only to be overwhelmed as they did so. Lee's army had lost nearly 4,000 dead and over 24,000 wounded and missing in the battle. If Meade had followed up his victory as he was ordered to do by Lincoln, there is no doubt that he could have destroyed the Confederate forces. Their retreat was blocked by the flooded Potomac and they were short of ammunition. The

Union army too had suffered sorely: 3,100 dead and 20,000 wounded—but they were not short of ammunition or reinforcements. It was paralysis in the command which delayed the pursuit; Meade seemed bemused at his success and procrastinated till it was too late. Lee was allowed to withdraw and escape with his entire army into Virginia. Except for Grant, Sherman and General George H. Thomas, the run of Union generals suffered from this excessive caution, 'this expanding and piling up of impedimenta which has so far been almost our ruin and will be our final ruin if it is not finally abandoned'.[8] When McClellan, Burnside and Hooker moved, they were lacking in bulldog determination to follow the enemy. Even Meade, having stood firm at Gettysburg, allowed Lee calmly to slip away undestroyed. All of them lacked the ruthless quality required by modern war and the American Civil War was certainly a war on a scale hitherto unknown. Yet the interesting fact is that despite the succession of defeats and failures throughout the first two and half years of war, the Union Army never failed to come back for more. Time and time again Lee severely damaged it, yet he had never destroyed its will or its capacity to fight again. The reason for this is partly the great resources of men and material mobilized by the North, but much more the iron determination of the President and Commander-in-Chief. However bad the news and however strong the spirit of defeatism on the home front, Lincoln never gave up. He constantly planned the next move, encouraged his generals and offered them his advice. It is well known that Lincoln suffered from moods of melancholy and depression, but whatever his personal feelings, he never allowed his will for victory to waver. Thus a single battle could not lose the war.

Lincoln had already spotted Grant as a general who was prepared to fight whatever the cost. In the middle of May 1863 Grant had settled down to besiege Vicksburg on the Mississippi. This strong fortified city was the bastion of the Con-

[8] It has been suggested that the over-caution and hesitation of many Northern generals came from their having been pupils at West Point when Lee was its Commandant. Grant and Sherman had never served under Lee.

federacy in the West: if it fell, the entire Mississippi would be under Union control and the Confederacy would be split in two. This had always been Lincoln's intention and he said that if Grant took Vicksburg, then 'He is my man and I am his for the rest of the war'. On July 4th, the day after Gettysburg, Vicksburg fell. Grant was appointed to full command of the armies in the West and in the following March was given supreme command of all the Union armies. He was exactly the general who could make full use of the great military machine created by trial, error and suffering in the first three years of war. With Grant at its head it was a machine which Lee found could no longer be turned aside from its purpose. It clung to the Confederate army in a bloody grip throughout the Battle of the Wilderness at Spotsylvania, and at Petersburg. Grant's blows were not those of a delicate swordsman; they were rather the bludgeon strokes of a battle-axe. They were expensive of men and material, but while the North could easily replace the loss it was by now beyond the powers of the Confederacy to do so. In one month, June 1864, Union losses amounted to nearly 60,000 men, almost the entire total of Lee's army. Confederate casualties were half. The struggle of Grant and Lee was an epic drama: modern total war faced the traditional conception of war as a contest of skill, finesse and chivalry. Lee, even if he had had the resources, could never have fought as Grant did. In the South-West the other side of total war showed itself, as General Sherman, having broken out of Tennessee, captured Atlanta and ravaged the economic resources of the Confederacy in his march to the sea. No longer was war simply to be waged against soldiers. By 1864 in fact, the Union Army and its strategy were revolutionary. It had been a slow revolution to achieve and its achievement owed much to Lincoln.

If Lincoln ultimately achieved his military intentions, he was also successful in his plan to blockade the South. As the army was virtually non-existent in 1861, so was the navy. It consisted of roughly ninety ships, a third of which were unseaworthy and the remainder were scattered in all parts of the world. Moreover the secession of Virginia meant the loss of the great naval yard at Norfolk. Lincoln had proclaimed a total blockade of the South in the early days of the war, but in order to enforce it every kind of craft of any size had to be recruited. An urgent building programme was started and within the year the blockade had become reasonably effective. Certain naval bases were established on the southern coast and the capture of New Orleans by amphibious operations greatly increased the efficiency of the blockade. Chances of capture were estimated in 1861 as one in ten; by 1864 it was one in three. Revolutionary ideas were not so necessary with the navy as with the army but in March 1862 a Confederate ironclad, *Virginia,* formerly the U.S.S. *Merrimac,* appeared at the mouth of the James and sank two Federal ships. This threat was met by another ironclad, the U.S.S. *Monitor,* developed experimentally from the plans of a Swedish engineer. A five-hour battle ended in a draw and the *Virginia* withdrew battered, later to be destroyed by the Confederates before Norfolk was recaptured by Union troops in May. It was the first fight between armoured vessels, a sign that on sea as on land modern war had come.

Apart from the vast military problem of equipping, financing and using a large army in aggressive strategical terms, Lincoln was also faced throughout his Presidency by political problems of vast magnitude. These problems concerned foreign affairs as well as political affairs at home. Lincoln realized that all military effort against the South would be wasted if the Confederacy were to be recognized by Great Britain and France. That this recognition would come was relied on by the Confederate leaders. European opinion already regarded the Union as irrevocably destroyed since it was generally held that the North could never conquer the South. Many British and French statesmen looked with favour on the disruption of the Union. It justified the view that Republics could not exist; it destroyed the increasing power of the United States (Great Britain in particular feared her rivalry in navigation); it opened up for France the prospect of success in the Mexican adventure planned by Napoleon III, since the Monroe Doctrine would be a dead letter. Indeed, if Europe had not taken the disruption of the Union as so inevitable, she might well have intervened. But Britain did not want war and France in her tightrope position in Europe could not afford to act without England's blessing. From the beginning the two powers agreed to act in concert on the American question.

The other major reason why Britain might intervene was 'King Cotton' and its vital importance in the British economy. The Confederacy deliberately held back the 1861 cotton crop in the belief that shortage of cotton would compel intervention. It failed to do so and as the war continued a clear division was seen between the views of the English governing classes and those of the middle and artisan classes. The former sympathized with the South but the latter favoured the North. They sympathized with democracy and disliked slavery. Merchants valued the markets of the North, manufacturers welcomed the cheap corn of the Middle West and the cotton workers showed themselves prepared to face unemployment as the price of freedom for the Negro slave. But in 1861 this division lay in the future and the new Republican administration faced the real danger of British intervention. Seward, as Secretary of State, was the director of American foreign policy and Lincoln supported him. His policy was in reality a gigantic bluff. It was simply to threaten Britain, from the very beginning, with war if one step were to be taken to recognize the South as an independent nation. In despatches, speeches and conversation Seward made this attitude clear. As William Howard Russell noted in his diary when he saw Seward:

> The Secretary then lit his cigar, gave one to me, and proceeded to read slowly and with marked emphasis a very long, strong and able dispatch, which he told me was to be read by Mr. Adams, the American minister in London, to Lord John Russell. It struck me that the tone of the paper was hostile, that there was an undercurrent of menace through it, and that it contained insinuations that Great Britain would interfere to split up the Republic if she could, and was pleased at the prospect of the dangers which threatened it.

Later Seward sent the famous Despatch No. 10, the bluntness of which had, in part, been toned down by Lincoln. Yet when Mr. Adams in London received it, it seemed 'almost to declare war with all the powers of Europe. I scarcely know how to understand Mr. Seward.' Adams was instructed to break off relations if Britain sought to mediate and he was told to say 'This is war' if certain naval rams being built for the Confederacy were allowed to sail. As a policy it appeared both mad and rash but it succeeded, as British diplomatic documents reveal. British statesmen felt certain that war would follow if they recognized the Confederacy, and it made them more cautious. Seward was an adept diplomat and, when occasion called, showed himself to be both adroit and moderate. The *Trent* affair in November 1861, when the two Confederate commissioners travelling to Europe were removed from a British ship after being stopped by an American warship, was well handled. Seward backed down by congratulating Great Britain on defending neutral rights as the United States had done in 1812 and averted almost certain war with Britain. When France intervened in Mexico (June 1863) Congress called for hostilities to maintain the Monroe Doctrine but Seward resisted the demand, realizing that the matter could well wait until after the Confederacy had been beaten. On both these occasions when war might have occurred Seward and Lincoln showed themselves to be accommodating. Only to prevent European intervention did they appear aggressive. It was indeed a masterly foreign policy. Above all, Lincoln showed himself to be an expert in publicity, indicating to the world by his speeches the real issue of the American Civil War: whether democracy could long endure.

In a sense the political problems at home were really the most important. For if the North could not be kept united, the will to win the war would fade. As it was, morale sank to a very low ebb on frequent occasions.[9] The trouble came from two main sources: the Democrats and the Radical Republicans. In the election of 1860 Stephen Douglas, the Northern Democrat, received 1,375,157 votes to Lincoln's 1,866,352. These Democrats had traditional links with the South and as the war proceeded many of them became more and more convinced that it was useless to pursue it. Lincoln had done what

[9] A good index of Union morale is the number of deserters and draft-dodgers from the army.

he could to enlist full Democratic support for the war by including Democrats in his Cabinet and by appointing them to military and civilian office. But as the long succession of Federal military failures continued, so the alliance was weakened. Moreover the Democrats bitterly resented the dictatorial power which the President appeared to be using. The suspension of Habeas Corpus, the suppression of newspapers, the detention of thousands of civilians confirmed their fears that the price of victory, even if it came, would be too high. The most aggressive of these Democrats were known as the Copperheads. Their centre was in the great Middle West—the States of Illinois, Indiana, Iowa and Ohio—which had voted solidly for Douglas in 1860. 'These are dark hours', wrote the Republican Senator Sumner in the black winter of 1862 after Fredericksburg. 'The President tells me that he now fears the fire in the rear [meaning the Democracy, especially of the North-West] more than our military chances.' It was this group led by Representative Clement L. Vallandigham of Ohio which engineered the Democratic nomination of McClellan in the Presidential election of 1864 on the platform that the war was a failure and that peace should be made. In the event it was unfortunate for them that before the election Sherman captured Atlanta and began his march to the sea, but even so McClellan gained 1,805,000 votes to Lincoln's 2,213,000. This was the measure of the danger. The Copperheads were simply a minority of active men but they had a great deal of passive support behind them. Throughout the war they remained a threat to morale, material and men.

The other political danger was of a different kind. It came from within the Republican party itself and was not opposed to the war. A group known as the Radicals had existed from the foundation of the Republican party and its leaders conceived of the war in totally different terms from Lincoln's. To them it was a crusade to end slavery, to establish the Negro as a free citizen with full social and political rights. These aims were subordinate to reconstruction of the Union, which was to take place only with the fulfilment of these conditions. To the Radicals the war was one to end slavery: to Lincoln it was one to preserve the Union. To the Radicals the Union had been dissolved by the secession of the Southern states: to Lincoln it was still in existence. The contrast is well shown in Lincoln's words, 'My paramount object in this struggle is to save the Union and it is not to save or destroy slavery', compared with those of Senator Charles Sumner: 'Remember. . . I am no idolator of the Union; I have never put our cause on this ground. But I hate slavery. . . .'

The Radicals in fact had at their core the old fanatical abolitionist spirit. Allied to it during the war were the forces of political intrigue and the greed of big business. This alliance was unconscious and many of the Radical leaders were idealists, burning with a righteous fervour of reform. But like many righteous movements it was made use of and, particularly in the period of Reconstruction, Radicalism became the instrument of political and economic ambition.

Their main strength lay in both Houses of Congress and from the beginning of Lincoln's administration they worked with increasing vindictiveness to impose their views. The leaders were Charles Sumner, Benjamin Wade, Zachariah Chandler, Joshua Giddings and Thaddeus Stevens. Within the Cabinet itself, which Lincoln had tried to make as representative as possible, they had allies in the Secretary of the Treasury, Salmon P. Chase, and the enigmatic Secretary of War, Edwin M. Stanton. Chase was a man of consuming political ambition who had hoped for the Presidency in 1860. His alliance with the Radicals was mainly designed to assist him in winning the Republican nomination in 1864. In December 1862 a Senatorial cabal attempted to break up the Cabinet by confronting Lincoln with a demand for Seward's resignation. They were sent away discomfited by the President's greater political astuteness. They resented not only Seward but also the Democratic generals, particularly McClellan, whom they bitterly attacked: 'McClellan in the field and Seward in the Cabinet have brought our grand cause to the very brink of death'. All military defeats were attributed to the fact that the generals were not Radicals.

More than anything else the Radicals resented the fact that slavery was not declared to be abolished at once. On August

30th, 1861, General John C. Frémont,[10] one of the Radical generals, had declared that all slaves of Missourians in rebellion against the United States were automatically free. Lincoln disavowed this order as he also did that of another Radical general, Hunter, in May 1862 when the slaves of Georgia, Florida and South Carolina were declared free. These disavowals infuriated the Radicals and, even when the Emancipation Proclamation finally came, it was far from satisfactory to them. In all these matters they found the President whom they despised to be adamant and they were forced to take what steps they could through Congress. They dominated the Joint Committee on the Conduct of the War which was created in December 1861. Its purpose was 'to keep an anxious watchful eye over all the executive agents who are carrying on the war at the direction of the people'. Senator Wade of Ohio was the chairman and under his direction the Committee harried the Executive Branch of the Government. To them all good generals were Radicals and despite the defeats of Frémont, McDowell and Rosecrans, they continued to acclaim their prowess. Any general who was a product of West Point was *ipso facto* anathema to them since he was supposed to be tarred with the pro-slavery brush. A prolonged campaign was carried on against the use of Presidential powers, a campaign which reached its ultimate conclusion in the impeachment of Andrew Johnson, Lincoln's successor as President. They objected bitterly to the suspension of Habeas Corpus and to the other measures taken to meet the emergency. They laid down policies about Negroes and about Reconstruction in every way opposed to those of Lincoln. No matter on which they could harry the Executive was forgotten or omitted. While Lincoln lived he was more than a match for them, although their activities placed an intolerable burden on him, in addition to those which are imposed on any war leader. On his death they entered into their kingdom and carried their policies of Radical Reconstruction.

[10] Frémont was a professional soldier who in the 1840's had carried out important explorations along the Oregon trail and the Arkansas, Rio Grande and Colorado rivers. Later he entered politics and was, as has been noted earlier, the first Republican contender for the Presidency in 1856.

There is no doubt that to look at the war from the Northern viewpoint, it is necessary to look at it through Lincoln. His purpose was to save the Union cause and at the same time to shape that cause in terms of eternal ideals and human values. In struggling towards this goal, he had to endure inefficiency, shameful greed, profiteering and factional bickering. Within the North he faced disloyalty from the Democrats and alarming division among the ranks of his own Republican party. In confronting and controlling these difficulties Lincoln became a statesman of the finest quality. The most remarkable achievement was that he avoided being possessed by 'the war mind'.[11] He never lost sight of the fact that he was fighting a war against other Americans whose ancestors had played a leading part in bringing forth 'on this continent a new nation, conceived in liberty and dedicated to the proposition that all men are created equal'. No one, as one contemporary observer noted, could fail 'to be impressed with his deep earnestness, his anxious contemplation of public affairs, and his thorough sense of the extraordinary responsibilities that were coming upon him'. His main feeling towards the war was one of deep regret that the avoidable tragedy had happened. As his Second Inaugural Address showed, he had a real sense of mystery as to the ways of Providence and a true understanding that the scourge of war was as much a punishment for the North as it was for the South. The North paid the price, not only in terms of human life but also in the rapid transformation of Northern society. Every great war results in a social and economic revolution and the American Civil war was no exception. In mobilizing the forces of the North, big business soon gained a vested interest in the conflict. The war from the Northern viewpoint involved a vast expansion of industry and in decades following it all aspects of American life were to be dominated by the values of big business.

Lincoln wanted the war to end with the surrenders on the battlefield. Healing and restoration were at once to take its

[11] As Professor David Knowles puts it: 'Lincoln could sympathize and yet act. He could pursue this end unswervingly, yet without a touch of that obstinacy and blindness which is the cause of the success of most strong men.'

place. His hopes were not to be realized but they are typical of the man and his greatness. It was a greatness built upon humanity; Lincoln the prairie lawyer was ambitious, he was humorous, he was sympathetic, he was firm. It was this humanity which was forgotten in his apotheosis after his death but it is the essential key to his greatness. Something of this quality comes from the farewell to his law partner William Herndon in February 1861 when he left Springfield for the last time.

Then he gathered up some books and papers, talked for a moment or so, and the two men walked downstairs together. At the bottom Lincoln glanced up at the battered law shingle. 'Let it hang there undisturbed,' he asked, lowering his voice. 'Give our clients to understand that the election of a President makes no change in the firm of Lincoln and Herndon. If I live I'm coming back sometime, and then we'll go right on practising law as if nothing had ever happened.'[12]

But something had happened, and because it had, the American Union was preserved.

[12] David Donald, *Lincoln's Herndon*, p. 147.

CHAPTER VIII

THE WAR FROM THE SOUTHERN
VIEWPOINT

Jefferson Davis, the President of the Confederacy, writing after the war, said in his massive apologia, *The Rise and Fall of the Confederate Government,* that 'the simple fact was the country had gone to war without counting the cost'. It is certainly true that few Southerners in 1861 conceived of a conflict of the type which ensued. Two illusions were prevalent. The first was that the North would not attempt coercion; if it did, the damned Yankees would easily be beaten and if they persisted in their folly, their economy would rapidly collapse under the strain. To the Southerner Cotton was King and since it provided the bulk of the American export trade the North would be unable to exist. The second illusion was also connected with the importance of cotton. European demands for cotton would bring speedy recognition of Southern independence and assistance from Great Britain and France. Both of these illusions affected strategy and diplomacy.

Besides illusions the South suffered from holding certain attitudes grounded on the fundamental belief in states' rights. The strategy to be adopted was to be one of defence since the South was simply defending its rights and should therefore not attack. Within the Confederacy itself a stubborn defence of states' rights was maintained throughout the war, particularly by Georgia and North Carolina under their Governors, Joseph Brown and Zebulon Vance. This led to constant bickering with the central government over the use of state troops, conscription, supplies and taxes. At times it almost appeared as if the individual states making up the Confederacy were prepared to lose the war, if the price of winning it were the surrender of the sovereign rights of individual states.

The constitution adopted at Montgomery in February 1861 for the Confederacy (then only seven states) was simply an adaptation of the old Federal constitution. Nothing could make clearer that the South was not fighting for some new political ideal. They were fighting to preserve the rights which to them appeared to be unprotected by Northern interpretations of the old constitution. The Confederate constitution merely emphasized the doctrine of states' rights: the President was elected for six years: Congress had no power to grant bounties, to impose a protective tariff or to levy an export tax except with a two-thirds majority. No money could be raised for internal improvements and the clause allowing Congress to provide for 'general welfare' was omitted. Finally state sovereignty was made explicit. The first President elected under this constitution was Jefferson Davis and it was to this man that the construction of the new government was due. An administration had to be organized, industries had to be started, an army raised and equipped. It was a colossal task and it would have been difficult at any time even without all the tensions of states' rights. In due course these tensions led to the greatest bitterness between the President and Congress, and between the President and individual states. Congress from the beginning was more of a sounding board for individual opinions and grievances than a responsible legislative assembly. It talked more than it acted and soon fell into a contempt which was reinforced by the scenes of violence which occurred there.

It has been suggested by his enemies that the Confederate epitaph should read 'Died of Davis'. He was a man who, unlike Lincoln, looked every inch a President, with a distinguished, well-formed head, thin lips and a goatee beard. He had never wished to be President and indeed would not have been elected but for a political muddle. Robert Toombs of Georgia was the obvious candidate; the other possible one was William L. Yancey but he was unacceptable since his fire-eating reputation would undoubtedly have offended Virginia, whose support the seven seceded states desperately hoped for. Davis wished to serve the Confederacy as a soldier and, indeed, he was well fitted to do so. Born in Kentucky in 1808 a few months before Lincoln and within a few miles of him, Davis had graduated from West Point and entered the Regular Army. He had served in the Black Hawk War (as Lincoln had done on a short-term engagement), and then resigned to become a planter in Mississippi with the help of his brother. In 1845 he was elected to Congress but resigned in the middle of his term to join the war against Mexico. Subsequently he was elected to the Senate, served as Secretary of War in the Cabinet of President Pierce and again became a senator. In the four years before the Civil War he was the most influential spokesman for the Southern cause in Congress. But although he had had plenty of political experience his real love was the Army.

It was unfortunate for the South in many ways that he became the President of the Confederacy. By 1861 his health was bad: he was blind in one eye and suffered from neuritis and dyspepsia, two complaints which did much to exacerbate his uneven temper. He was a man of high principles and character, with a pronounced sense of public duty, but he lacked the common touch. He made little effort to court popularity and his personality was incapable of generating warmth or enthusiasm. Unwilling to make concessions once he believed in a certain course of action or policy, in his whole manner he appeared both prickly and unbending. People must agree with him in order to get along with him. Once his loyalty was given, he stuck to it firmly as he did with Lee and with his Secretary of State, Benjamin. His rigidity was most conspicuous in his interpretation of the prerogatives of his office which he maintained down to the last comma. This precise insistence on the letter of the law was unfortunate in the context of states' rights and the emphasis put upon them in the South. In Davis then the South had a man of indomitable will, who, while he had not sought the Presidency, was resolved to give it the last ounce of his devotion. Regrettably his character was not one to emotionalize a people and as the months passed Davis became a hateful figure to a large number of Southerners. Inevitably the pressures of war required a strong executive and the President soon represented the centralizing tendency in government which was hateful to the tradition of the South. By 1863 certain Southern leaders seemed willing to lose the war rather than surrender to a strong central control, which if adopted at the outset might have won the war.

In appointing his Cabinet Davis was guided by geographical and political considerations. The Secretary of State was Toombs of Georgia, soon to be replaced by Hunter of Virginia and then by Benjamin of Louisiana, formerly the Attorney-General and Secretary of War. Memminger of South Carolina was Secretary of the Treasury, Mallory of Florida Secretary of the Navy and Reagen of Texas the Postmaster-General. The Secretaryship of War was successively held by Walker of Alabama, Benjamin and finally Seddon of Virginia. All of these men were unfortunately professional politicians, many of them narrowed by the bitterness of pre-war politics. Davis would have been wise to seek talent from a wider field. Moreover, despite the attempt to create a representative Cabinet its main characteristic was that its members were men of the New South. They did not represent the planter aristocracy of the Old South. Most were men of humble origin; Memminger had been born in Germany and had spent his childhood in a Charleston orphanage; Mallory's father had come from Connecticut and having moved to Florida died, leaving his widow to make ends meet by running a boarding house. Benjamin was the son of a London fishmonger.[1]

The Old South in fact provided little political talent for the Confederacy. In the first thirty years of the original Union the Old South, personified by Virginia, had contributed many great statesmen; four of the first five Presidents alone came from the State of Virginia. But during the Civil War this tradition of leadership was almost entirely confined to the Army. Robert E. Lee, Stonewall Jackson, Jeb Stuart, Joseph E. Johnston from Virginia and James Longstreet from Georgia—these are the great names of Confederate generals. It was left to the New South to find the statesmen. No one today remembers

---

[1] After the fall of the Confederacy, Benjamin returned to England where he took up law most successfully, becoming a Queen's Counsel and writing an important book on the law of Sale.

heir names as he does those of the Northern Cabinet; they
have left few stories or sayings behind them. Yet the Confederate generals are household names with a glamour which is not
simply that of a defeated cause. Except for Grant and Sherman, Northern generals are relatively unknown. Southern generalship was infinitely better than that of the Northern right
to the closing months of the war, whereas the Union Armies
floundered in their leadership until the last year. History has
paid tribute, as it usually does, to success. The same is true
in the civilian field; Southern statesmanship was woefully mis-
ed, whereas under Lincoln the North was conspicuously successful. The Old South in fact gave the Confederacy the mili-
ary prestige which glamorizes the whole cause; the politicians
who failed are largely forgotten men.

Davis did not require that his Cabinet should take a vital
and forceful part in planning or formulating policy. Their job
was to administer their departments; and even in this Davis
often interfered through his conscientiousness, overtiring himself with unnecessary detail. Only with Benjamin was he on
terms of close friendship and he had a high regard for his
advice (except on finance). With the others he was often high-
handed. When Hunter was Secretary of War he received a
crushing rebuke from Davis on opening his mouth to voice an
opinion: 'Mr. Hunter, you are Secretary of War and when in-
formation is wished of that department it will be time for you
to speak'.

Nevertheless this Cabinet did succeed in achieving an enormous amount and it should be remembered that it was done
under the tensions of war and not in the relative tranquillity
of peace. For nearly four years armies totalling in all over a
million men were kept in the field, somehow armed, supplied
and fed. It was a nightmarish task considering the bareness of
Southern resources. The move of the capital to Richmond in
Virginia from Montgomery in Alabama was explained by its
symbolic importance as the heart of the 'Old Dominion' and
also by the value of retaining this area so rich in supplies for
the hard-pressed Confederate government. Foundries had to
be made from scratch, nitre beds created for gunpowder, factories started for cloth and horses recruited for cavalry. The

main organizer of this task was the Quartermaster-Genera
Josiah Gorgas, a man of outstanding capacity. The seizure c
Federal arsenals at the beginning of the conflict had provide
a certain foundation, and throughout the war the capture c
Federal supplies provided an invaluable addition. But fron
1863 onwards the gap between what was required and wha
was available had become too wide. The railway system of th
South in 1861 was inadequate, covering only 9,000 miles, cor
siderably less than a half of the mileage available to the Nortl
With a little energy the system could have been much in
proved by providing links between vital junctions. But Cor
gress at first refused to appropriate money to aid a privat
company since 'this would establish executive tyranny an
would be a violation of the constitution and the rights of th
States'. Thus a forty-mile link between Danville and Greens
boro, North Carolina, was not finished until May 1864 an
Atlanta was never provided with a link at all between th
various railroads meeting there. Moreover the South suffere
from a variety of gauges varying from three to six feet, an
this entailed endless unloading and reshipment.

Inadequate supplies and an insufficient transport syster
whose rolling stock deteriorated rapidly meant that the South
ern armies were always in want. Their achievements on th
field of battle are all the more remarkable in view of this
The despatches of Confederate generals are filled with com
plaints of shortages in every direction, including men. In Apr
1862 the government had passed a conscription Act, draftin
all white men between 18 and 35 for a period of three years
There was a long list of exempted occupations; teaching, fo
example, became a popular occupation. Many state leader
questioned the legality of the Act and did everything to defea
it; in North Carolina over 25,000 men were officially classe
as state officials, thus securing exemption. Desertions from th
Army mounted as the war continued. In the summer of 186;
Davis received from Lee the message that 'the number of de
sertions from the army is so great and still continues to sucl
an extent that unless some cessation of them can be caused
fear success in the field will be seriously endangered'.

Desertions came not only from conditions at the front bu

so from soldiers' anxieties for their families at home. To keep
e armies in the field supplied, however inadequately, meant
at the home front had to be deprived of everything. Southern
rms were mainly left in charge of old men and women. Re-
arkably the slaves remained completely loyal[2] although pro-
action inevitably suffered from the lack of active young
utherners. The blockade resulted in a desperate shortage
both luxuries and necessities: medicines, salt, clothing, nee-
es. Manufactured articles of every kind were soon unobtain-
le and Southern women were forced to contrive substitutes.
ithout doubt the suffering was considerable and in the de-
ine of Southern morale the effect of letters from home to
ldiers in the armies must not be underestimated.

The struggle of Jefferson Davis and his Cabinet was not sim-
ly with material difficulties but also with political difficulties
home. As a body the Confederate Congress was a disap-
ointment and spent much of its time quarrelling and talking.
y the end of 1864 the reputation of Congress was at its lowest
ob. 'If a goose served for a sentinel when Rome was to be
efended, why should not a Congressman be fitted for the
me duty when the capital of the Confederacy is beleaguered?'
rote one disillusioned Richmond editor. Congress often at-
cked the President and his Cabinet but it never harassed
e Confederate Executive as much as the United States Con-
ress did that of Lincoln through the Joint Committee on the
onduct of the War. The really damaging attacks on the Con-
derate administration came from the state Governors. Brown
Georgia and Vance of North Carolina found no occasion
no incident too petty to ignore and it has been said of them
y one historian that 'they did perhaps as much as Grant or
herman to destroy the Southern Confederacy'. Over the con-
cription law a bitter fight was waged between Davis and
rown which the latter finally carried into a pamphlet war.
cannot consent', he proclaimed, 'to commit the State to a

[2] This fact is often used by Southerners in defending the South.
ost slaves did not suffer greatly under slavery and they had both
ffection and respect for the good master and his family. As a so-
ial system slavery undoubtedly had its advantages, but it was a
atic system providing no path to eventual freedom.

policy which is in my judgement subversive of her sovereign
and at war with all the principles for the support of whi
Georgia entered into this Revolution'. Davis's actions we
those of a 'military despotism' converting Georgians 'into va
sals of the Central power'. The Governors of Alabama, Miss
sippi and Texas eventually aligned themselves with Brown
the issue of conscription, and Governor Clark of Mississippi v
tually threatened to go to war against the Confederacy. 'I sh
be compelled to protect my State officers with all the forc
of the State at my command.' The fight over conscription ce
tred on the writ of Habeas Corpus, the suspension of whi
was the most effective way of enforcing conscription, th
maintaining the strength of the Confederate Army. It was ty
cal of the political troubles which dogged Davis. His on
chance of avoiding this constant bickering was to have reco
nized the power of states' rights and to have made use of
If he could have created an advisory council of Governors a
associated them directly with the formation of Confedera
policy, he might have prevented the vindictive quarrels whi
did so much to sap the Confederacy of its morale. The politic
division within the Confederate states is a sign that the Sou
in its political theory was as out of step with the modern wor
as it was over slavery.

Besides political and material difficulties there were al
grave economic troubles. The root cause of these was fina
cial. When Memminger became Secretary of the Treasury
had to make initial payments out of his own resources sin
the Confederate government possessed none. In all during fo
years of war he scraped together 25 million dollars of speci
calling finally on women's jewellery, wedding rings and fami
treasures. How insignificant this total was, can be seen whe
it is set against the fact that in 1864 the Federal governme
was spending over 25 million dollars in eight days. The re
financing of the Confederacy in fact was not done by spec
but by paper. All through the war currency was issued fro
the printing press in ever-increasing quantities, both by t
Confederate government and by the individual states. On
journalist described the portraits appearing on Confedera
banknotes by commenting on 'that unchanging expression

effable melancholy which the engraver has given to all of
them; for on the best specimens of Confederate currency Davis
doleful and Stephens saturnine, Hunter is heavy, Clay
ouded with care, and Memminger is mournful'. Well might
they appear careworn and mournful as they witnessed infla-
on riddling the Confederacy. Cheap money led to high
rices: in 1863 one comment by a Southerner was that 'it
ould cost fifty dollars to get tight here'; by 1864 a cup of
offee cost five dollars and a lady's bonnet three hundred dol-
rs. This inflation caused speculation, extortion and corrup-
on and did much to undermine public morale. Innumerable
adly printed pieces of paper, bearing the words 'The Con-
derate States of America will pay to the bearer on demand
. .' played a large part in the downfall of the Confederacy.

No attempt was made to evolve a proper taxation system.
y following the original Federal constitution it was impossi-
le to levy direct taxes without apportioning them to popu-
tion and no census was taken. Export taxes could not be
aised except with a two-thirds majority and anyway there was
o export trade. Various attempts were made to devise peri-
dic taxes of one kind and another, but throughout its existence
he Confederacy only raised one per cent of its income in taxes.
nstead it relied on paper money and this had no backing ex-
ept the credit of the government. Through a woeful miscal-
ulation of statesmanship the Confederate government had
issed a unique opportunity of establishing its credit on a se-
ure financial foundation. In 1861 the cotton planters of the
outh had millions of bales of cotton on their hands which
hey would gladly have exchanged for Confederate bonds. The
reasury could then have shipped the cotton to Europe and
n the large cash balances thus acquired have established its
nancial security beyond question. One hundred thousand
ales would have produced fifty million dollars. Twenty times
his amount could easily have been shipped to Europe in the
irst year of the war. The Northern blockade was largely in-
ffective at this time since Lincoln had less than a dozen ships
o enforce a blockade of a coastline 3,500 miles long. But the
Confederate government held the great illusion that 'Cotton
vas King'. Not one bale of cotton must be shipped to Europe

while Europe refused to recognize Southern independence. /
cotton famine in Europe would be the most effective mear
of securing a speedy end to the war. In pursuit of this polic
Davis decreed a cotton embargo; no ship was to leave th
South for Europe. This embargo was ruthlessly enforced wit
vigilance committees standing guard at the ports.

Seldom does history disclose a blunder of statesmanship s
monstrous. Cotton was indeed King in a different sense to th
one understood by the Confederate leaders. If it had bee
shipped to Europe it could have been made the solid founda
tion of the Confederacy, providing a firm rock of financial an
economic power. As it was the retention of cotton within th
South had no influence on British and French policy. Bot
countries possessed considerable stocks of cotton and by th
time these were used up, public opinion in Britain had swum
to the North as the middle and working classes began to re
alize the issues of the war. Hostility to slavery and support fo
democracy were stronger forces than the threat of unemploy
ment, apparently due to a shortage of cotton. The Souther
commissioners to Britain and France were soon speedily dis
illusioned. James M. Mason in London and John Slidell i
Paris, having reached their destinations after their original se
zure from the *Trent*, were left in no doubt that however sym
pathetic political leaders might be in private conversatior
they were not prepared to take public action.[3] Napoleon II
would have liked to do so but he could not act without Britis
approval.

Slidell made an attempt to use the power of cotton afte
the Confederate government realized its original mistake. Thi
attempt was the famous d'Erlanger loan. A bond issue was t
be launched by the French banking firm for fifteen millio

[3] In fact the British government came near to recognition in th
autumn of 1862. Lord John Russell wrote to Palmerston on Sep
tember 17th: 'I agree with you that the time is come for offerin
mediation to the United States Government with a view to th
recognition of the independence of the Confederates. I agree fu
ther, that in case of failure, we ought ourselves, to recognize th
Southern States as an independent State.' On the same day th
battle of Antietam was fought and Lee withdrew to Virginia. Thi
news restrained the British government from action.

dollars secured on Confederate cotton at twelve cents a pound. This valuation was absurdly low since if the cotton could once reach Europe it would fetch five times the price. Interest on the bonds was to be seven per cent and d'Erlanger's were to buy them at 23 points below par of a 100. The issue of bonds was made in March 1863 and was at first well received. But before settling day, when subscribers were required to pay the full amount of their purchase, the price of the bonds on the Paris Bourse began to fall steadily. D'Erlanger's threatened to withdraw from the whole operation unless the Confederate commissioners allowed them to strengthen the market. This was to be done by using the instalment money of fifteen per cent, already subscribed by purchasers, to buy up bonds on the Bourse. Of the eight and a half million dollars available over six million was spent in this way. It was all in vain since in July came the news of Gettysburg. The market collapsed. D'Erlanger's had been shrewd enough to sell the major portion of their own holdings. The eventual result gave the Confederacy only two and a half million dollars and d'Erlanger's received about the same amount. It was a financial fiasco which made all the more bitter the original miscalculation on the power of cotton.

The Confederacy failed by threats to persuade Britain and France to intervene. It failed also to do so with its promises to assist France's adventure in Mexico. Its attempts to sway public opinion in its favour were also a failure; journalists and leader writers employed in London wrote article after article in vain. No European power recognized the Confederacy as an independent state except for Poland (itself unrecognized) and the Duke of Saxe-Coburg-Gotha. One wit suggested that the seal of the new nation should carry the picture of a man paddling his own canoe with the motto 'Damn England and France'. Bereft of foreign support, the Southern states were left to secure their independence by their own exertions.

Most Southerners were wildly over-confident in the early months of the war and believed that the North would speedily be defeated by the superiority of Southern manhood. 'The race is not to the swift, nor the battle to the strong' was some consolation from the words of Holy Writ, if consolation were

needed for anyone sufficiently perceptive to realize that th
war might not end quickly. In terms of resources the Soutl
was vastly inferior to the North,[4] but the war might be wo
if a rapid attack were made before Northern manpower and
manufactures could make themselves felt. Unfortunately, th
aggressive general strategy which might have gotten the vic
tory was woefully lacking. This failure was originally due t
the illusions that the North would not, and then could not
fight (First Bull Run), and that European recognition would
be forthcoming. In terms of these illusions the war was re
garded as purely defensive, and the official strategy adopted
by Davis was one of 'ditching and digging'. The demand by
certain politicians and generals for a major advance on Wash
ington after the battle of First Bull Run was not kindly received
by the Executive. When one looks at the mobility of Jackson
in the Valley campaign of 1862 and at Lee's invasion of the
North in the Antietam and Gettysburg campaigns, one won
ders what would have been the result if offence had dominated
the counsels of the Confederacy at the outset. But Davis and
his Cabinet were not offensively minded. As one Richmond
editor sarcastically expressed it: 'This man Jackson must be
suppressed or else he will change the humane and Christian
policy of the war and demoralize the government. Evidently
he has lost his mind. Down with him or he will establish the
independence of the Southern Confederacy.'

Equally, if they had adopted the policy of ruthless retalia
tion which Sherman was to pursue in the last year of the war,
victory might have come nearer. But most Southern generals
were gentlemen brought up to believe that war was chivalrous,
with nothing retaliatory, destructive or total about it. The
earlier Union generals had confirmed Lee in his belief that the
war was to be fought on these terms; he was shocked and

[4]	North	South
Population	22 million	9 million (3½ million slaves)
Railways	21,700 miles	9,000 miles
Value of manufactured Products	$1,700 million	$156 million
Production of Corn	717 million bushels	316 million bushels
Production of Iron	480,000 tons	31,000 tons

appalled when confronted by the brutal military machine directed by Grant and Sherman which obeyed no code of chivalry or of gentlemanly behaviour except in the hour of final victory.

Even when the earlier illusions had evaporated, the Confederacy never worked out a general strategy for the whole war. There was never an offensive concentration of forces, which in view of the manpower problem was a lamentable mistake. Instead the overriding doctrine of states' rights led to a wide dispersal of troops in order to protect individual states. The only real permanent concentration of troops was in Lee's Army of Northern Virginia around Richmond. Lee was a brilliant tactician; his battles have always delighted military scientists and have remained a subject of compulsory reading for army cadets to the present day. But he always refused to consider the strategy of the war as a whole and his friend and loyal supporter Jefferson Davis was content that he should not do so.

Lee was an individualist and indeed individuality was the mark of Southerners. They were not used to working as a team and this trait characterized both the civilian and the military effort in the war. To Lee his job was to command a particular army and to win the particular battle before him. He did not view the war as a whole or analyse the problem that the South would have to win the war quickly if it were to win it at all. In his terms an honourable draw would be sufficient. Born of a Virginian family long distinguished in colonial history and with a father who had taken a prominent part in the revolutionary war, he had entered West Point and been commissioned in the Engineers. He had seen active service in the Mexican war and had commanded a cavalry regiment on frontier duty in Texas. In 1859 he had sprung into the public eye when he commanded the troops which suppressed John Brown's raid. Given command of the Army of Northern Virginia in June 1862, he had shown himself vastly superior to the Union generals opposing him. He removed McClellan's threat to Richmond in the Seven Days' Battles (June 25th–July 1st, 1862) and had achieved triumphant successes at Fredericksburg and Chancellorsville. Greater determination to press his advantage home

might have brought victorious results. His invasion of Pennsylvania and repulse at Gettysburg mark the turning-point o
the war.

His career was a monument not to intellect but to principle
His character was beyond reproach and he became the focu
of Confederate morale. He radiated confidence and his nea
figure on horseback was a source of inspiration to the mex
who never failed him. Disliking slavery, he had joined Virginia
from a sense of duty and throughout his life he was upheld
by a belief in God; he did the best he could and left the rest
to Heaven. After the war was over he dedicated himself to
the task of doing what he could to restore the shattered South
He showed no bitterness and by his example did much to
reconcile Southerners to the harshness of defeat. To one mother
who brought her infant son to him and asked for some words
of guidance he replied: 'Madam, teach him to deny himself'
This was certainly the lesson of his own life and just as Lincoln
represents all that was best in the Northern side so Lee appeared to personify the type of aristocratic greatness which
was the ideal of the South. Neither man was ever captured
by the 'war mind'. Lee was the simpler character of the two
and at the end of the four years of bloodshed it can truthfully
be said 'he stood in the centre of the crimson field but without
a drop of blood on his hands'. He was a remarkable figure of
great simplicity, austerity and integrity of character, who in
his own life time grew into a man of the ages.

His conception of generalship was, having once made a plan,
to allow his subordinates to carry it out without interference
from him. His reserve made familiarity with him unthinkable
and his courtesy certainly made him too considerate of his subordinates. This reliance on an individual once he had given
his confidence to him was often an undoubted weakness. At
Gettysburg his tolerance of Longstreet's prevarications was
disastrous but on balance it can be held that Lee's trust in his
subordinates gave encouragement to initiative. As the commanding general he was always prepared to take the blame
for anything which went wrong. After Gettysburg he repeated,
'Tell them it is all my fault', and he never hesitated to accept

responsibility.[5] Both as a commander in the field and as a general viewing the war in its entirety Lee lacked the qualities of ruthlessness and determination which might have made him a greater general but which would have made him a lesser man. In the long run Lee gave to the Confederate cause a distinction which colours it to this day. If the price of victory required a sacrifice of principles and character it was a price Lee was incapable of paying.

Lee's army was the one major concentration of forces in the Confederacy. A grand strategy for the war might have made a similar concentration along the Mississippi and kept that vital line intact. Instead individual states were allowed to retain forces within their own borders, ignoring the fact that with the Mississippi lost the Confederacy was split in two. Surprisingly Davis paid little attention to the New South which had done most to bring about the war. It was always held as secondary to the Old South, to whose retention the most sustained military endeavour was devoted. Vicksburg and Gettysburg mark the real end of any possible hope that the Confederacy could win the war. In November 1863 the Union victories at Chattanooga (Lookout Mountain and Missionary Ridge) left them in a position to bisect the Confederacy horizontally by marching through Georgia to the sea. Lee's efforts for the last fifteen months of the war became increasingly unrealistic when set in the context of what was happening elsewhere. Even if he could have repulsed Grant, the war was already lost as the other Union armies won control of the remainder of the Confederacy.

The historical conclusion about the military side of the war from the Southern viewpoint is that if an aggressive policy had been pursued from the outset, the chances of decisive military victory were strong. If Washington had been seized in 1862, the North would have lacked the will to wage war. As it was the South threw away its aces from theories and illusions.

[5] When his army was finally surrounded in April 1865 he refused the easy way out of engaging in a heroic but useless final battle. 'Then there is nothing left for me to do but to go and see General Grant, and I would rather die a thousand deaths.'

After July 1863 tactical skill could not overcome the stubborn facts of brutal and total war.

What conclusions then can be reached about the Confeder ate failure to win Southern independence? Died of Davis, died of illusions, died of states' rights—none of these are wholly sat isfactory as explanations. The answer surely lies in the failure of the Southern people to give the kind of self-sacrifice which the struggle demanded. One old Confederate soldier put it 'We have courage, woodcraft, consummate horsemanship and endurance of pain equal to the Indians but that we will not submit to discipline. We will not take care of things, or hus band our resources. Where we are, there is waste and destruc tion. If it could be done by one wild desperate dash we would do it.' No wild desperate dash had been permitted and as the war proceeded the South as a whole showed itself unable to accept the sacrifices demanded by the war. There was plenty of material self-sacrifice but Southerners showed themselves incapable of the right kind of political imagination. States clung to their rights, individuals to theirs. The failure to equip the railway system to meet the needs of the time was typical. The statesmen of the South were unable to overcome this obstinate insistence on rights, an obstinacy created in the long years of racial tension before the war. Jefferson Davis failed, in fact, to create a nation as Gladstone rashly held that he had done.[6]

There is no escaping the feeling that the whole creation of the Confederacy was a mistake. A majority of Southerners had not been willing to break up the Union, but had followed their states into secession unwillingly. In this sense the Vice-Presi dent Alexander Stephens is the most symbolic character in the history of the Confederacy. He was a small, withered figure of great intellectual powers who had done his best by his elo quence to keep his State of Georgia from secession. He ac cepted the office of Vice-President unwillingly and after the

[6] Gladstone, speaking in Newcastle upon Tyne, October 7th 1862: 'There is no doubt that Jefferson Davis and other leaders of the South have made an army; they are making, it appears, a navy; and they have made what is more than either, they have made a nation'.

first few months refused to visit Richmond except occasionally. In his heart he regarded the Confederacy as a mistake. In March 1865 he headed the Southern delegation to the fruitless Hampton Roads Conference to discuss peace. His terms of reference laid down by Davis were 'to negotiate for the purpose of securing peace to the two countries'. Stephens wanted to discuss 'the conditions under constitutional safeguards for the return of the South to the Union'. Here at the very end, a month before Appomattox, was the same clash out of which the Confederacy had been born. It was the clash between Southern nationalist and states' rights Unionist. Davis, even as Lee was approaching the moment of surrender, clung to the ideal of a Southern nation. It was an ideal which had never become a reality. 'What are you going to do?' asked Davis on the Vice-President's return from Hampton Roads. 'I intend to go home and remain there,' replied Stephens. This indeed was the fundamental tragedy of the Confederacy: that home to most Southerners was their state within the Union, and many beside Stephens regretted that they had ever become prodigal sons.

CHAPTER IX

RECONSTRUCTION

The problem of Reconstruction was not a new one arising only after the defeat of the South in battle. In the decades before the Civil War the South had been setting itself apart from the North in the intellectual, social and religious spheres of life. Southerners ceased to send their sons to Harvard, Yale or Princeton; they ceased to spend holidays at Northern centres such as Saratoga Springs; Northern magazines, actors, musicians no longer appeared in Southern towns. The South, in fact, increasingly withdrew itself into a romanticized life of its own, relying on its own social and cultural resources. In religion the split had been definite; the Methodist Church of the South separated as early as 1844 and a year later the Baptist Church divided on the same issue of the propriety of moral agitation against slavery. Secession had raised the problem of political Reconstruction and the war had severed the economic ties which linked the North to the South. Reconstruction, therefore, in the fullest sense means the process by which the South was brought back into the Union, intellectually, socially, politically, economically and spiritually.

Confederate veterans returning to their houses found a ruined land. Apart from the material devastation the whole basis of Southern economic life had been disrupted. Confederate money was worthless and the freeing of slaves by the 13th Amendment meant that the bulk of Southern capital disappeared. Plantations were overgrown and there was no labour force to work them. Even if the ex-slaves, often bewildered and intoxicated by their new-found freedom, were prepared to work, their former owners had no money with which to pay them. Before long an answer was found by the system of 'share cropping' tenancy. The Negro and the poor white rented a

parcel of land, were provided with seeds and tools and in return gave to the landlord a share of the resulting crop. This
system had its defects; in particular it usually meant that the
tenant was kept permanently in debt, and was liable to concentrate on only one type of crop in order to gain the quickest
return irrespective of the exhaustion of the land. Yet it was
probably the best answer to the immediate economic problem
of the South and it provided an economic framework within
which white and Negro could live together. Thoughtful
Southerners realized the need to diversify their economy and
at first welcomed the infusion of Northern capital into their
economic life. Unfortunately, Northern capitalists were unscrupulous in their search for industrial opportunities in the pros-
trate South. They picked up bargains in Southern railroads,
timber and coal. By the late seventies the South had learnt its
lesson; it must help itself. Thousands of Southerners then began to contribute capital from their slender resources to start
factories and iron mills. In the course of time man's natural
resilience reasserted itself; by 1870 as much cotton was being
produced as in 1860 and by 1890 the yield had doubled. By
1900 the manufactured products of the South were four times
as much as in 1860. By itself it was a remarkable achievement
and only appears insignificant when compared to the staggering industrial advance of the rest of the country.

It was over political Reconstruction that most bitterness was
engendered. Lincoln in his Second Inaugural had asked that
'with malice toward none, with charity for all. . . . Let us
strive on to finish the work we are in, to bind up the nation's
wounds', and his spirit of reconciliation was answered by many
Southern leaders in the words of Robert E. Lee: 'The war being at an end . . . I believe it to be the duty of every one to
unite in the restoration of the country, and the re-establishment
of peace and harmony'. Unfortunately, Lincoln's policy was
not followed. The Radical Republicans instead imposed a
policy on the South which has been described by one Southerner as 'a deliberate attempt to humiliate the people who had
lost everything by the war, and it aroused passions on both
sides that were unknown when the war was in actual progress'.

Idealists among the Radicals, on the other hand, claimed

to be making a genuine attempt to give justice to the Negroes by guaranteeing to them the full democratic rights to which they were entitled. But whatever the intention, the result of this policy was that the South continued for a long time to regard their political reconnection with the Union as something forced and inevitable rather than as something desirable, while the Negro was left unnecessarily lamed in his move towards political and social freedom.

Lincoln's policy before Sumter had been based on the hope of a peaceful Reconstruction of the Union through Southern Unionist sentiment. Out of this hope developed Lincoln's war policy towards Reconstruction. He held that the Union had not been dissolved by the act of secession; it remained in existence whatever individual states may have said and done. Therefore, as the Union armies occupied Southern states, some scheme of political action had to be formulated to enable the seceded states to become once more active partners in the Union. In December 1863 Lincoln announced his plan for Reconstruction. Citizens who had been qualified voters in 1860 must take an oath of loyalty to the constitution and the Union. They could then vote for a state convention which must pass legislation against secession and slavery. Having done this they could reconstitute the ordinary political machinery of the state. Lincoln only required one-tenth of the 1860 electorate to take the oath for a state to be re-admitted to the Union. His plan did not ask for any positive action towards the Negro beyond emancipation. Once he was freed, his status was regarded as the particular concern of each individual state.

Louisiana and Arkansas fulfilled the required conditions in 1864 but Congress refused to admit their representatives to the Senate and the House. Here was the root of the trouble; Congress, dominated by the Radical Republicans, claimed that Reconstruction was its responsibility and not that of the President. The Radicals were naturally violently opposed to Lincoln's generous scheme. They held that the Union had been dissolved by secession and agreed either with Thaddeus Stevens that the South was conquered territory or with Charles Sumner that the seceded states had committed suicide. On either counts Reconstruction was a matter for Congress; it should be carried out in a manner clearly emphasizing that the South had lost the war and that the Negro was now guaranteed full political and social equality. Some of the Radicals were idealists like Sumner but many of them were simply shrewd politicians who saw the advantages for the Republican party in enfranchising the Negro.

The Presidential election of 1864 had shown the power of Northern Democracy.[1] Republicans might well fear defeat if the Southern states were restored with full voting rights and with increased representation in Congress, the Negroes being now counted as full citizens. That these fears were well grounded was shown in the election of 1868 when General Grant, the greatest living Northern hero, polled 3,012,883 votes to the Democratic candidate's 2,703,249. Grant's victory in fact was due to the success of the Radical policy in the South by which six Southern states were dominated by 'carpet-bag'[2] governments and three states were not yet re-admitted to the Union.

The Radicals had shown their opposition to Lincoln's policy as early as 1864 by passing the Wade-Davis bill. This required the majority of the electorate in a seceded state to take an oath abjuring the past, before the state could be considered for restoration to the Union. Lincoln vetoed this bill, an action greeted by a chorus of insult from the Radicals. After Lincoln's assassination his successor, Andrew Johnson, showed that he intended to continue in the general direction set by his predecessor. By December 1865 every Confederate state except Texas had fulfilled Lincoln's conditions for re-admission to the Union and their representatives arrived in Washington to be met by a Congress which flatly refused to endorse the President's actions. A Joint Committee of the two Houses was established to pass judgement on the qualifications of the Southerners and this Committee was dominated by the Radicals. Under its direction Congress laid down new conditions for the admission of the 'conquered provinces' and set up Freedman's Bureau to take care of the freed slaves. This organization which

[1] See p. 127.
[2] A type of valise used by Northern travellers; the phrase was applied indiscriminately to all new-comers to the post-war South.

did a great deal of good in helping the Negro was to become the stronghold of Radical policies in the South.

It cannot be denied that the Southern states had openly flouted both Northern opinion and Johnson's advice by adopting special laws known as the 'Black Codes' for the control of the former slaves. To preserve the South as a white man's country was the avowed aim of the white majority[3] and under Lincoln's scheme for Reconstruction they possessed freedom to act as they liked. Lincoln was always a realist and, while it is regrettable, it is not surprising that the South acted as it did. Outsiders who do not have to live with the problem of race are in no position to impose a policy with any confidence that the people directly concerned will accept it. Southern whites could not suddenly accept the Negroes as their brothers. Despite Johnson's suggestions that literate Negroes should be given political rights, nothing was done, and the Black Codes regulated the mobility of the Negro by requiring him to make a long-term contract with an employer on pain of being arrested for vagrancy if he did not do so. All of this was a spur to justifiable Radical indignation and Congress passed the 14th Amendment in June 1866. This amendment virtually contained the Radical programme for reconstructing the Union. It declared that all people born or naturalized in the United States were equal citizens both of the Union and of their individual state: no state could deprive any citizen of 'life, liberty or property without due process of law'[4] or deny 'the equal protection of the laws'; any state denying any of its citizens the right to vote would have its Congressional representation proportionately reduced[5]; any former Confederates who had held Federal or state office before the Civil War were barred from holding such office again unless Congress removed such disability by a two-thirds majority; and finally the South's responsibility for its share in the public debt of the United States was underlined and any attempt to repay the debts of the Confederacy was

[3] But see p. 160, below.

[4] This clause later became extremely important in protecting firms from state taxation, though not intended for this purpose.

[5] Since Negroes now counted as full citizens the three-fifths rule of Article I Section 2 of the constitution was overruled.

forbidden. This amendment emphasizes the greatly increased power of the Federal government as a result of the war. Previously the rights of citizenship and voting had been largely a matter for individual states. For the first time rules had now been formulated which states must follow. Ratification of the 14th Amendment was made a condition for the readmission of the Southern states and almost all of them at first refused to submit. Only Tennessee at once ratified the amendment; the other states hoped that the coming mid-term Congressional elections would defeat the Radical control of Congress. These hopes were disappointed. By waving 'the bloody shirt'[6] and by pointing out that the South was unrepentant the Republican party swept the elections. Race riots in New Orleans and Memphis helped to support their argument. With a more than two-thirds majority in both houses of Congress the Radicals were in a position to carry out their policy.

The new Congress at once passed a series of Reconstruction Acts treating the Southern states as conquered territory, divided into five military districts each under a Major-General. These commanders were charged with the duty of setting up new governments in which Negroes were guaranteed the right to vote. Ex-Confederates were denied the franchise and military courts were set up to decide disputes. Under this military régime Radical Reconstruction proceeded apace. By the beginning of 1868 Radical-dominated governments in the Southern states were in control. Known as 'carpet-bag' governments, after the nickname given to Yankee agents, they quickly ratified the 14th Amendment and by July seven of the former Confederate states had been re-admitted to the Union. The 15th Amendment was then proposed forbidding any state from depriving a citizen of his vote because of 'race, colour or previous condition of servitude'.

It has been reckoned that under Radical Reconstruction 700,000 Negroes had the vote compared with 625,000 whites. This meant that in every state a 'carpet-bag' government was at some time in control. Inevitably these governments tended to be inefficient and corrupt. Negro leaders were largely un-

---

[6] A phrase describing Republican emphasis on the cost of war to suppress the rebellion in terms of dead and wounded.

educated and on many occasions were the dupes of Northern agents. They had little financial sense and many state governments recklessly granted concessions to Northern business firms and raised loans to finance projects of little merit.[7] State debts mounted and white property owners who had to bear the taxes were driven to deep resentment. Yet these governments can claim a credit balance: legal reforms, constitutional improvements, the establishment of public schools and colleges for Negroes, support the claim that given time all would have been well. But whatever can be said to the credit of the 'carpet-baggers', their real effect was to convince the Southern whites that the Negroes were unfit for political power and that the Republican party was beyond the pale. Radical Reconstruction created the solid Democratic South.

In order to push through its policy Congress showed itself to be quite unscrupulous about the safeguards of the constitution. In designing the constitution, the Founding Fathers had sought to prevent any one branch of the government from overwhelming the rest.[8] The Supreme Court was one safeguard. The Radicals feared that the Court would declare their Reconstruction Acts to be unconstitutional and the Court was therefore forbidden to pass any opinion on them. To prevent President Johnson from intervening Congress laid down that when a Supreme Court Justice died no replacement was to be made. Johnson was a man of courage but of little tact who attempted to do his duty as the constitution laid down. He was prepared to enforce the Reconstruction Acts but attempted to limit their operation within the strict bounds of the constitution. With their majority the Radicals were in a position to override his veto, but this was insufficient for them. Intoxicated with power, it was intolerable to them to have a President such as Johnson standing in their way. They passed an Army Act requiring the President as Commander-in-Chief

[7] The greatest financial extravagance was, however, in states where the legislature was dominated by upstart whites.

[8] All nations of the western world in the late 19th century began to emphasize the doctrine of national sovereignty. The increased power of the Federal government after the Civil War is therefore in a sense an assertion of the fact of sovereignty against the political theory of the constitution.

to issue orders only through the General of the Army. This was followed by the Tenure of Office Act forbidding the President to dismiss officers appointed with the advice and consent of the Senate unless he had senatorial approval. Johnson believed this Act to be unconstitutional and he decided to face the issue by dismissing Edwin Stanton, the Secretary of War. This was the signal for the Radicals to join together for the kill. They impeached Johnson before the Senate for 'a high misdemeanour' and after a trial of intense excitement failed to remove him from office by one vote short of the necessary two-thirds majority.

This blatant use of the weapon of impeachment in the interest of a political clique had its effect on thoughtful opinion in the North. If the Republicans had not nominated Grant as their Presidential candidate for 1868, the reaction against Radical Reconstruction might have set in earlier than it did. But the combination of the victorious General beneath the banner of 'the bloody shirt' maintained a Republican administration in power, and Reconstruction continued. Already however the Southern whites had begun to fight back. With Federal troops in their midst this could not be done openly but secret societies sprang up, the most notorious of which, the Ku Klux Klan, was founded in 1867. Recruits were sworn to secrecy and members of the Klan pursued their activities at night in the disguise of hoods and white robes. 'Carpet-baggers' and Negroes were frightened by threats and violence. The Klan ultimately became so brutal that it was suppressed, but not before it and its fellow organizations had succeeded in driving the Negro away from the polling booth. Gradually white conservatism reasserted control over Southern governments and by 1876 only Florida, South Carolina and Louisiana remained in the hands of carpet-baggers. In the Presidential election of that year the Democratic candidate, Samuel J. Tilden of New York, came within an inch of victory. The reaction against Radical policies and the corruption of the Grant administration[9] had

[9] Grant was an inept and naïve politician. In his Presidency big business bought politicians to obtain concessions. The whisky ring involving Grant's private secretary and the impeachment of the Secretary of War for receiving bribes are typical examples of the

resulted in a striking Democratic success. Rutherford B. Hayes of Ohio, the Republican candidate, could only win the election if the disputed election returns in the three states still under Radical rule were decided in his favour. Tension mounted and cries were heard from Northern Democrats that Civil War would come again. Fortunately good sense prevailed and Republican and Democratic leaders in Congress reached an unwritten compromise. This compromise marked the end of Radical Reconstruction. Hayes was allowed to win the election in return for the withdrawal of all Federal troops from the South. A Southerner was to be appointed to the Cabinet and more Federal funds were to be made available to improve Southern transport and finance a railroad from New Orleans to the Pacific. It was not only good sense which brought about this settlement; it was also good business. Northern and Southern property-owners felt that a new era had come in which 'the bloody shirt' had no place. Sectional interests came once more into alliance and the traditional system of compromise and bargaining between sections (whose breakdown had caused the Civil War) was re-established.

Radical Reconstruction was a tragic mistake with lasting consequences. By ignoring the social problem of the Negro it aroused burning bitterness among Southerners and made them believe that they had been treated much more harshly than they actually were. No Southern leader had his property confiscated and despite demands 'to hang Jeff Davis on a sour apple tree', the only people executed after the war were the assassins of Lincoln and the officer in command of the Confederate prison camp at Andersonville. Inevitably the South had to suffer after the war; the economic devastation alone and the liquidation of capital in the emancipation of the slaves made this inescapable. Radical Reconstruction combined with the financial policies of the 'carpet-bag' governments added humiliation and further economic hardship. It was this humiliation which the South could not readily forget or forgive. As a result the South, while it lost by defeat its states' rights theory of the constitution, in many ways won a victory over the

corruption which discredited Grant's Presidency. It can be paralleled by the scandals of the Harding administration, 1921–23.

North regarding the status of the Negro. The outcome of the Civil War was to free the slave but the outcome of Reconstruction was in the long run to confirm the tradition of white supremacy over the black race.

Yet it is a mistake to think that the South at once adopted harsh and vindictive policies towards the Negro. In the problem of race relations the South has never stood still. C. Vann Woodward, in a series of lectures entitled *The strange career of Jim Crow,* has shown convincingly that segregation of white and Negro was not the immediate result of Reconstruction. Segregation of the races had never existed before the Civil War and it was established only in a limited way in the Black Codes during the years of Reconstruction. After 1877 there was no great eagerness to expand it. Southern conservatives held that while the Negro was a subordinate, there was no reason to segregate or humiliate him. The conservatives sought to attract the Negro vote by a paternalistic policy of protection akin to the best side of the former slavery system. Southern Radicals, the leaders of the Populist movement in the South, attempted for their part to enlist Negro support on the basis of community of interest: 'the coloured tenant . . . is in the same boat with the white tenant, the coloured labourer with the white labourer . . . the accident of colour can make no difference in the interests of farmers, croppers and labourers'. Both parties flattered the Negro for their own political ambitions and neither recommended policies of proscription, segregation and disfranchisement. These policies only triumphed at the end of the century when the struggle of conservatives and radicals ended in a stalemate. Frustrated and economically depressed, the South looked for a scapegoat, and found him in the Negro. To reconcile the bitterness between themselves the whites adopted a policy of absolute white supremacy. The legend of Reconstruction was revived and was used to defend policies of segregation and disfranchisement. In an ugly atmosphere of hate and vengeance certain conventional attitudes about the Negro said to date from the period of Reconstruction were renovated: he was generally unfit to vote; the only hope for good and efficient government in the South rested upon the political supremacy of the white; and the Negro was better off under this system. Within twenty years segregation was made almost universal throughout the South and a series of 'Jim Crow' laws[10] marked the triumph of a narrow racial policy which had little to do with the experience of Civil War and Reconstruction. It is only in recent years that the South has begun to revise this policy.

The problem of race, as Lincoln realized, allows of no easy solution. Neither does it permit ease of historical judgement. Not until the publication in 1935 of W. E. B. Du Bois's *Black Reconstruction* was an attempt made to look at Reconstruction from the Negro's point of view. Du Bois argues that the Negro was never given a fair chance; most Northerners had not fought the war to end slavery and the idealists among the Radical Republicans were too few in number to control the selfish and material interests of the North. These interests were prepared to make terms with the Southern whites in 1877 and by so doing delivered the Negro to his former master. The hopes and dreams of the freedman were thereby stifled while his achievements in the period of Reconstruction were largely ignored. A stereotype of the Negro emerged from the experience of these years; he was ignorant, lazy, dishonest and extravagant, and he was responsible for bad government in the South after the Civil War.

It is undoubtedly true that a general unanimity exists in regarding the Reconstruction era as a tragic one. Given ideal conditions, the patience to guide slowly, the willingness to accept sacrifice, it is certain that the Negro could have been brought to full citizenship and responsibility. But conditions are never ideal and the generation after the Civil War was not prepared to accept patience or sacrifice. Southerners were determined to keep the South a white man's country by one means or another and the majority of Northerners were not prepared to force the issue. Reconstruction was involved also with political and economic pressures among the whites and

[10] These laws were fuller than the Black Codes and much more rigorously enforced. They established racial segregation in churches, schools, housing, jobs, eating, sports, public transport, hospitals, orphanages, prisons, asylums and finally in funeral houses and cemeteries.

the Negro inevitably suffered. As Du Bois has shown the achievement of several Negro-dominated states was considerable and this achievement has been hidden behind the general charge of corruption and extravagance, in the same way as the reputation of Negro leaders has been blackened by their association with 'carpet-baggers'. With time and goodwill the achievement would have established itself and the Negro would have reached the full citizenship to which he is entitled. What happened was indeed a failure of American democracy, but it happened. In the circumstances of the post-Civil War decades it was bound to happen. In this sense, historical judgement is correct in condemning Reconstruction as a tragic mistake. So was the Civil War, but the war came.

Politically, nothing could have done so little to aid the task of reconciliation as Radical Reconstruction. It founded the tradition of the Solid South which always voted Democratic and it was not until the Presidential election of 1952 that this tradition was broken. In the period after the Civil War politics were sterile. This was partly because politicians who had failed to prevent the war continued to conduct politics on a narrow pre-war sectional basis. New forces were transforming the United States in the decade after the war; industry, trade and transport were undergoing vast expansion and it was in these fields that ambitious young men poured out their energies. Politics offered no such opportunity since the activity of the major political parties remained rigidly fixed in patterns established by the bitter controversies of the Civil War and Reconstruction. Ancient watchwords inappropriate to modern issues and out-of-date alignments unresponsive to new demands dominated the thinking and the actions of the parties. The 'bloody shirt' continued to be waved in election after election by Republicans although as early as 1872 a group known as the Liberal Republicans reacted against it. Their leaders were such men as Lincoln's former Secretary of the Navy, Gideon Welles; Horace Greeley, the famous editor of the *New York Tribune;* and Carl Schurz, a progressive politician from Wisconsin. In the 1872 Presidential election the group joined with the Democrats to nominate Greeley for the Presidency. Despite this revolt, the 'bloody shirt' was retained as a political slogan long after the passions of the war had died down. The average man continued to vote from habit without much thought about the candidates, many of whom had little vision and less constructive ability. The persistence with which the 'bloody shirt' was waved disguised the fact that reconciliation in many other fields was having conspicuous success.

In 1884 a baby born in the year of Gettysburg could vote without having any memory of slavery or the Civil War. Nearly two-fifths of the voting population by 1888 was under thirty years of age and only a quarter of the whole electorate had possessed a vote in 1860. No senator had sat in the Senate before 1856. When Jefferson Davis died in 1889 he had been preceded to his grave by his Vice-President, by three-quarters of his Cabinet and by most of the signers of the Confederate constitution. A new generation had arrived and old issues were dying with the men who had given them life. Before his death Jefferson Davis had been able to say in a public speech:

> The past is dead; let it bury its dead, its hope and its aspirations; before you lies the future, a future of golden promise a future of expanding national glory. . . . Let me beseech you to lay aside all rancour, all bitter sectional feeling, and to make your place in the ranks of those who will bring about a consummation devoutly to be wished— a reunited country.

If one's eyes are taken away from politics a remarkable progress in the Reconstruction and reconciliation of national life can be seen. Business men, railway entrepreneurs, tourists, novelists, journalists all played their part in weaving together again the strands of a common Americanism in both North and South. Within a generation true peace came to those who had been at war, although in the first ten years after Appomattox it seemed as if bitterness was ineradicable. Incidents of Union soldiers standing guard to prevent flowers being cast on Confederate graves or the howl of hate demanding Jefferson Davis's execution were typical. The words of the Southern Presbyterian Minister in 1870 echoed in many a Southern home: 'I do not forgive, I try not to forgive. What, forgive those people who have invaded our country, burned our cities, destroyed our homes, slain our young men? No, I do not forgive them.'

Ten years later the change of attitude is already remarkable. By 1881, twenty years after Sumter, veterans of both sides were meeting to rejoice that they were no longer foes. In 1888 at the Gettysburg reunion all the soldiers of the Blue and the Grey cheered the speaker who said: 'Today there are no victors, no vanquished. As Americans, we may all claim a common share . . . in the new America born on this battlefield.' The motto of this new America was indeed Lincoln's Gettysburg address. To this generation the war began to be surrounded by a haze of sentiment and romance. Novelists and poets began to romanticize the Old South—a South of faithful black mammies, gracious ladies, courteous gentlemen, stately homes and mint juleps. This romantic tradition in a way became a fact, giving to Southern youth a foundation upon which to build a new life of courage and energy. To the present day the South has had a peculiar contribution to make to American life. It is the one section of America which has tasted defeat and failure and this is an experience wholly foreign to the general pattern of American history. To a certain extent, the sense of its romantic past has enabled the South to retain a hold on values which prosperous and successful America has usually rejected. The North, too, came to appreciate, through the tradition painted of the Old South by novelists and poets, something of the reasons which made so many Southerners prepared to fight and die for 'Dixie'.

To the men of the new generation to live for the new America, expanding in every direction, was better than to live in the memories of the past. If politicians were slow to do so, so much the worse for them. In this respect the Civil War marked the great divide in American history. Political issues relatively ceased to be important, whereas the enormous growth in industry, business and immigration dominated men's minds and energy. The great heroes were no longer politicians but millionaires like Andrew Carnegie, John D. Rockefeller, Cornelius Vanderbilt, whose names are successively linked with the development of steel, oil and railways. The Great West was opened up to farming and each year hordes of

Europeans passed through American ports providing cheap labour and an expanding market. In the penultimate decade of the 19th century more than five and a half million immigrants entered the United States. To such men the Civil War was simply an historical fact of little relevance to their new life. The forces transforming America spoke of the future not of the past.

Out of the suffering and cost of four years of war the Union had been preserved. Some historians argue that the war was a mistake and that if Sumter had not occurred the Union would have been reconstructed in course of time. This judgement ignores the folly, wickedness and stupidity of men which permit of no accurate forecast of events. Judgement must be made on events as they happened, not on what might have been. The war at least made certain that the Union was maintained, that the slaves were freed, and that a democratic republic had shown its power to live, however inadequately for some of its citizens. Thomas Jefferson in his First Inaugural Address had said:

> some honest men fear that a Republican government cannot be strong; that this government is not strong enough. But would the honest patriot, in the full tide of successful experiment, abandon a government which has so far kept us free and firm, on the theoretic and visionary fear that this government, the world's best hope, may by possibility want energy to preserve itself?

The North under Lincoln had given to the world a decisive answer to this question, even though Europe had felt that the Union must be destroyed and the Confederacy had felt that victory was certain. Lincoln thus confounded the doubters. He brought the American Union through its gravest test and in so doing established the strength of the democratic ideal. He also confirmed the continuity of American history, since the Union designed by the Founding Fathers emerged triumphant from the ordeal of the Civil War. The sense of being a chosen people was strengthened. The war had been fought not so much to destroy the constitution as to establish one interpretation of it against another. High though the cost had been in terms

of suffering and loss, Americans began to judge that the price
had not been too high for what was gained. The Civil War became a matter of pride, not one of shame and regret. Men on
both sides had risen to the occasion and acted nobly for their
beliefs. As one New Englander put it in 1901:

> Every man in the eleven States seceding from the
> Union had in 1861, whether he would or no, to decide for
> himself whether to adhere to his State or to his nation;
> and I finally assert that whichever way he decided, if only
> he decided honestly, putting self-interest behind him, he
> decided right.

Thus in a generation was the verdict of events—the triumph
of the Union—accepted. The heroes of North and South, of
the Blue and the Grey, became national heroes. Both sides
acted as they did because they could do no other. In its way
the blood shed in the war sanctified and strengthened the
Union for later generations of Americans. To think otherwise
is really to be un-American. For in the Civil War the United
States became a nation. To over-emphasize the evils and lost
opportunities of Reconstruction is to forget this fact. Once
again we are faced by the clarity of Lincoln's vision. He saw,
what historians have been slow to accept, that in the years
1861–65 America was engaged in a great Civil War, testing
whether a nation conceived in liberty could long endure. Shall
we not also accept his verdict on the causes and consequences
of that war: 'that the judgements of the Lord are true and
righteous altogether'? If we agree with Lincoln's conclusions,
we can hold that the Civil War, unlike so many conflicts, was
not all pain and loss. Judging the war today in terms of the
interests of the American Union we can say:

> *Nothing is here for tears, nothing to wail*
> *Or knock the breast; no weakness, no contempt,*
> *Dispraise or blame.*

TIME CHART

1787   North West ordinance for the territory north of Ohio River. Slavery prohibited.

1788   Sept. U.S. constitution declared to be ratified.

1790   Congress organized the South-West territory allowing slavery.

1804   Louisiana Purchase by President Jefferson for 15 million dollars.

1808   Jan. Importation of slaves prohibited by Congress.

1817   American Colonization Society founded.

1820   Missouri Compromise.

1831   First issue of *The Liberator* edited by William Lloyd Garrison.

1832   Nullification crisis.

1833   American Anti-slavery Society founded.

1836   'Gag' rule adopted in Congress to prevent abolitionist publicity by petitions.

1840   Liberty party candidate received 7059 votes in Presidential election.

1846   War with Mexico.

1848   Treaty of Guadalupe Hidalgo by which Mexico relinquished claims to Texas and ceded the territories of California and New Mexico. In Presidential election the Free Soil party made up of anti-slavery Democrats, New England Whigs and Liberty party nominated Van Buren. He obtained only 291,263 votes in total poll of 1,871,908.

1850   Compromise of 1850.

1852   *Uncle Tom's Cabin* by Harriet Beecher Stowe published.

1854   Kansas–Nebraska Act.
       July. Formation of the Republican party.

1856   'Bleeding Kansas.'
       Brooks's attack on Sumner in the Senate.
       In Presidential election Republican candidate Frémont gained 1,335,264 votes to Buchanan's 1,838,169.

1857   Dred Scott decision.

1858   The Lincoln–Douglas debates.

1859   John Brown's raid.

1860   May. Democratic convention split.

In Presidential election the Republican candidate Abraham Lincoln was elected.

20 Dec. South Carolina seceded.

1861   Jan.–1 Feb. Six further Southern states seceded.

4 March. Lincoln's inauguration.

12 April. Attack on Fort Sumter.

15 April. Lincoln's call for 75,000 volunteers to suppress the insurrection.

17 April–21 May. Four Border states seceded.

21 July. First Battle of Bull Run.

Nov. Seizure of Southern commissioners from the *Trent*.

20 Dec. Joint Congressional Committee on the Conduct of the War.

1862   9 March. *Monitor* v. *Merrimac*.

17 March. McClellan's embarkation for Peninsula began.

23 March–9 June. Jackson's valley campaign.

6 April. Battle of Shiloh.

26 April. Occupation of New Orleans.

26 June–7 July. Seven Days' Battle.

30 Aug. Second Battle of Bull Run.

17 Sept. Battle of Antietam turned back Lee's invasion of Maryland.

13 Dec. Battle of Fredericksburg.

1863   1 Jan. Emancipation Proclamation.

2–4 May. Battle of Chancellorsville.

1–3 July. Battle of Gettysburg turned back Lee's invasion of Pennsylvania.

4 July. Surrender of Vicksburg.

20 Sept. Battle of Chickamauga.

23–25 Nov. Battles of Lookout Mountain and Missionary Ridge.

8 Dec. Lincoln announced his plans for Reconstruction.

1864   5 May–3 June. Battles of The Wilderness, Spotsylvania and Cold Harbour.

2 Sept. Occupation of Atlanta by Sherman.

In Presidential election Lincoln was re-elected.

22 Dec. Sherman occupied Savannah.

1865   3 Feb. Hampton Roads conference.

4 April. Lincoln's second Inaugural.

9 April. Lee surrendered at Appomattox.

14 April. Assassination of Lincoln.

1865   26 May. Last Confederate army surrendered.

29 May–13 July. Johnson organized provisional government for seven states.

4 Dec. Congress met and set up Joint Committee of fifteen to deal with Reconstruction.

18 Dec. 13th Amendment abolishing slavery formally proclaimed in effect.

1866   May. Ku Klux Klan founded.

16 June. 14th Amendment drawn up.

20 June. Report of Joint Committee of fifteen.

Nov. Congressional elections giving Radicals more than two-thirds of each house.

1867   March. First Reconstruction Act passed over Johnson's veto. Military Reconstruction.

1868   16 May. Johnson's impeachment defeated by one vote.

In Presidential election Grant elected.

1869   Feb. 15th Amendment drawn up.

1872   In Presidential election Liberal Republicans and Northern Democrats nominated Greeley.

1876   Deadlock in Presidential election between Hayes and Tilden led to compromise by which 'Black Reconstruction' of the South was ended.

BOOKS FOR FURTHER READING

Books on the American Civil War are numbered by the thousand. Many of them are over 500 pages long and inevitably daunt the most enthusiastic English reader. Interpretations of the Civil War, as I have tried to show in my introductory chapter, were formed in the first two post-war decades, and increased research has done little to vary them. The following list of books attempts to give some guidance along the well-beaten tracks of what might appear to be a jungle. In recent years most of these books have become obtainable in England and all of them can be borrowed from the American Library, Grosvenor Square, London.

Interpretation

Daniel J. Boorstin, *The Genius of American Politics*, provides a stimulating study of the American political tradition: chapter 4, 'The Civil War and the Spirit of Compromise', is particularly valuable. Thomas J. Pressly, *Americans interpret their Civil War*, examines the changing pattern of interpretation. A shorter examination by Howard K. Beale appears in 'Theory and Practice in Historical Study', a report of the Committee on Historiography (Social Science Research Council). David M. Potter, 'The Lincoln Theme and American National Historiography', is a perceptive and witty lecture on the subject, as is P. Geyl, 'The American War and its Inevitability' (*New England Quarterly*, June 1951).

General Works on the approach to the Civil War

Allan Nevins, *Ordeal of the Union* (2 vols.) and *The Emergence of Lincoln* (2 vols.) are invaluable. The best single volume on the whole period is J. G. Randall, *The Civil War and Reconstruction*. G. F. Milton, *The Eve of Conflict*, and Avery O. Craven, *The Repressible Conflict, 1830–61*, examine the period from the view that the war was a needless one. *Nationalism and Sectionalism in America, 1775–1877* (select problems in historical interpretation), ed. D. M. Potter and T. G. Manning, gives an unsurpassed selection of extracts, both from contemporary sources and from historians. Also valuable are the volumes in the series published by Amherst College entitled 'Problems in American Civilization':

The Compromise of 1850; Slavery as a Cause of the Civil War; Lincoln and the Coming of the Civil War.

The Constitution and Political Parties

Max Farrand, *The Making of the Constitution,* and W. E. Binkley, *American Political Parties; their Natural History,* both provide straightforward accounts of their subjects.

The Frontier and Sectionalism

F. J. Turner, *The Frontier in American History* and *Sections in American History,* are the two classic books. His *Rise of the New West* elaborates the former. Charles S. Sydnor, *The Development of Southern Sectionalism, 1819–1848,* and W. E. Dodd, *The Cotton Kingdom,* trace the change in the South's views towards nationalism. 'Sectionalism and the Civil War', by Maldwyn Jones in *British Essays in American History* (ed. H. C. Allen and C. P. Hill), is an excellent short study.

Slavery and Abolition

U. B. Phillips, *American Negro Slavery,* is the most comprehensive examination of slavery as it existed in the South. K. M. Stampp, *The Peculiar Institution,* emphasizes the value of slavery as a method of dealing with the problem of race. A. F. Tyler, *Freedom's Ferment,* G. H. Barnes, *The Anti-slavery Impulse, 1830–1844,* and Dwight L. Dumond, *Anti-slavery Origins of the Civil War in the United States of America,* cover the abolition movement from every point of view.

The contemporary journals of F. L. Olmsted give a magnificent picture of southern life; these were edited in one volume by A. M. Schlesinger in 1953. W. D. Cash, *The Mind of the South,* provides a penetrating analysis (available as a paperback in England).

Compromise and its Failure

This subject is covered by the general works on the approach to the Civil War. In addition, R. F. Nichols, *The Disruption of Democracy,* James C. Malin, *John Brown and the Legend of Fifty Six,* and R. A. Billington, *The Protestant Crusade, 1800–1860,* are valuable.

The Cause of Secession

Avery O. Craven, *Edmund Ruffin, Southerner, a Study in Secession,* Dwight L. Dumond, *The Secession Movement, 1860–1861,* are probably the two best books. There are numerous studies of the individual secession movements in Southern states. A. C. Cole, 'Lincoln's Election, an immediate Menace to Slavery in the States?' (*American Historical Review*, Vol. 36), and J. G. Hamilton's article of the same title in Vol. 37 present opposite views.

The Cause of War

D. M. Potter, *Lincoln and his Party in the Secession Crisis*, examines the events before Sumter in detail. J. G. Randall's essay, 'Lincoln's Sumter Dilemma', appears in his *Lincoln the Liberal Statesman*. A vivid contemporary account of the last days of peace comes in William Howard Russell, *My Civil War Diary*.

The War from the Northern and Southern Viewpoints

(1) *Military.* The best general history of the war is Bruce Catton, *This Hallowed Ground*. C. E. R. Henderson, *Stonewall Jackson and the American Civil War*, is a classic. So is D. S. Freeman, *R. E. Lee* (4 vols.). This is biography written on the grand scale and Freeman attempts to write about each battle as if he were in the same 'fog of war' as Lee. To read these volumes is a memorable experience. From the Northern side the best book is T. Harry Williams, *Lincoln and his Generals*. In two volumes there is Kenneth P. Williams, *Lincoln finds a General*. The life of the ordinary soldier is well portrayed in Bell I. Wiley, *The Life of Johnny Reb* and *The Life of Billy Yank*.

(2) *Political.* Lincoln's political troubles are best described in T. Harry Williams, *Lincoln and the Radicals*, and Wood Gray, *The Hidden Civil War, the Story of the Copperheads*. Foreign policy is dealt with in Jay Monaghan, *Diplomat in Carpet Slippers*.

For the Confederacy, Burton J. Hendrick, *Statesmen of the Lost Cause*, E. M. Coulter, *The Confederate States of America, 1861–1865*, and Charles W. Ramsdell, *Behind the Lines in the Southern Confederacy*, cover most aspects. F. L. Owsley, *King Cotton Diplomacy*, is the best study of Confederate diplomacy.

Reconstruction

The best general summary is to be found in J. G. Randall, *The Civil War and Reconstruction*. Paul H. Buck, *The Road to Reunion, 1865–1900*, deals with Reconstruction in intellectual, social and moral life. W. E. B. Du Bois considers Reconstruction from the Negro's point of view in *Black Reconstruction*. E. M. Coulter, *The South during Reconstruction, 1865–77*, is a fair survey from the

Southern point of view. The Radicals are condemned in C. G. Bowers's *The Tragic Era*, written in a racy journalistic style. The same can be said of G. F. Milton, *The Age of Hate*. C. Vann Woodward, *Reunion and Reaction*, deals with the Compromise of 1877; he seeks to show that the business interests of North and South, allied before the Civil War, renewed the alliance to bring an end to political bitterness. His book, *The Strange Career of Jim Crow*, examines the general development of racial policies in the South. Louis M. Hacker, *The Triumph of American Capitalism*, elaborates the thesis of Charles and Mary Beard that Reconstruction was part of the attempt by Northern capitalism to control the nation.

Biography

Lincoln is obviously the great figure for Civil War biography. Many of the early biographies were amateur and unscholarly. It fell to Lord Charnwood, an Englishman, to write the first life (1916), which considered Lincoln as a figure of universal and not simply of American importance. An Englishman also wrote the first short study of the Civil War which revealed a compassionate and universal understanding of the issues and personalities involved. Professor David Knowles published his book in 1926 and it has unfortunately been out of print for some years. In admitting his fascination for the Civil War as a subject, this eminent medieval scholar concluded that Lincoln was 'the man who, above all others in modern times, has gone far to solve the deep moral problems underlying the exercise of power over others. . . . The possession of power only made him gentler and humbler than he had been before, and years of the greatest strain seem to have developed his charity as well as his ability. He is unique among men of action . . . he is the supreme example of the American character, the new blood by which the world has been enriched in the new world beyond the seas.' The best one-volume life today is B. P. Thomas, *Abraham Lincoln*. J. G. Randall, *Lincoln* (4 vols.), and Carl Sandburg, *Lincoln the Prairie Years* (2 vols.) and *The War Years* (2 vols.), are the most authoritative if the most dissimilar recent biographies by Americans. Sandburg's four volumes have been compressed into one which was published in England by Jonathan Cape (1955).

Except for D. S. Freeman, *R. E. Lee*, no great biography has appeared on other Civil War leaders. The following, however, are well worth reading: R. Korngold, *Thaddeus Stevens*, R. von

Abele, *Alexander H. Stephens*, W. E. Dodd, *Jefferson Davis*, W. E. Woodward, *Meet General Grant*, Liddell Hart, *Sherman*. David Donald is shortly producing a life of Charles Sumner.

Fiction

It is natural that the great experience of the Civil War should provide a recurring theme for novelists. T. Nelson, *The Sin of the Prophet,* deals with abolitionist feeling in New England, while Harriet Beecher Stowe, *Uncle Tom's Cabin,* is a classic contemporary novel inspired by abolitionist propaganda. J. C. Harris, *Uncle Remus,* and Mark Twain, *Huckleberry Finn,* give an attractive and humorous picture of Negro life under slavery. L. Ehrlichs, *God's Angry Man,* portrays John Brown. The classic story about the war itself is Stephen Crane, *The Red Badge of Courage.* This has been made into a film as has Margaret Mitchell's *Gone with the Wind,* a story of Georgia during the war and Reconstruction. G. W. Cable, *John March, Southerner,* deals with Reconstruction politics. Stephen Vincent Benét's poem, *John Brown's Body,* is a superb epic of the whole struggle and should be read at all costs.

Illustrations

The magazine *American Heritage* provides many articles on the Civil War authoritatively written and profusely illustrated. Recently an American publishing house has made available *The Photographic History of the Civil War.* Before this new edition appeared it was extremely difficult to obtain this superb record. It contains nearly 4000 photographs, rather indifferently reproduced, and draws heavily on the work of the famous Civil War photographer, Mathew Brady. By itself it is probably the best means of exciting interest in the most fascinating event in American history. A one-volume book *Divided We Fought* (general editor David Donald) contains an excellent selection of photographs with a high standard of reproduction.

INDEX

ANCHOR BOOKS

AMERICAN HISTORY AND STUDIES

2Ab